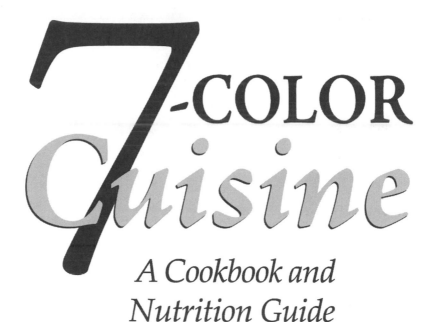

7-COLOR Cuisine

A Cookbook and Nutrition Guide

MARCIA ZIMMERMAN

SQUAREONE
PUBLISHERS

COVER DESIGNER: Jeff Potter
PHOTOS BY: Karen Sinell and Kannen Studios

To learn more about Marcia Zimmerman and her work,
visit her website at **www.marciazimmerman.com**

Square One Publishers
115 Herricks Road
Garden City Park, NY 11040
(516) 535-2010 • (877) 900-BOOK

www.squareonepublishers.com

Printed in Canada
ISBN 978-0-7570-0209-0

10   9   8   7   6   5   4   3   2   1

Contents

With special gratitude I dedicate this book to my dad, Arthur Stone, who taught me how to make meals a feast for the eyes, a treat for the palate and nourishment for the soul. Always beside my dad was my mom, Hazel Stone, whose love and guidance made meal preparation something to be enjoyed. My grandparents, Miriam and Peter Rey, were always part of our very close family and I owe them so much for believing in me. My grandmother's recipes are still some of my favorites.

Preface

My *Dad* Taught Me to Cook?

THE INSPIRATION for this cookbook has been a passion for enjoying good food made with superior ingredients, many of them just picked. It has taken me a long time to realize that my unusual early experience with food taught me the basics of what I'm sharing with you in this book.

Surprisingly, my early culinary experience came from the joys of eating really good, rich ice cream—mocha chocolate chip being my favorite—and freshly baked cherry pie. My parents and grand-parents owned a thriving soda fountain in the Haight-Ashbury district of San Francisco during the late 1940s. My dad was one of the best "soda jerks" around, plus he was artistry in motion as he moved with purpose from freezer to mixers to syrup dispensers, never missing a beat. He could unfailingly remember who wanted to skip the nuts on top of their sundaes or get double helpings of cherries. His spotless stainless steel environment evidenced the quality of what he served. People came to watch my dad, some peering through the plate glass window as they waited outside for a seat at the counter where it was always crowded with people enjoying their favorite sundae, soda, or milk shake. Some people took home hand-packed quarts of ice cream for a special treat. My dad and grandfather always added a little extra scoop so you could barely close the top of the carton. No prepacked ice cream cartons found their way into our store!

We served a limited menu, primarily a classic American hamburger (3-inch diameter, not a Whopper) made from the leanest, freshest beef, topped with my mother's classic tomato sauce and accompanied by thick, golden French fries that had been hand-peeled and cut. My grandmother's fresh pies were legendary, and she also presided over a fine breakfast menu that included home-made pastries and wonderfully farm-fresh eggs and bacon.

This first phase of my love affair with food is the basis for my simple four-step plan to eating well. It includes becoming well organized, using only top-quality unadulterated ingredients, loving and mindful preparation, and inspiring presentation—just like my dad's ice cream creations, which were true works of art.

The second phase of my culinary education brought me to the farm, where I learned firsthand about growing and enjoying the freshest fruits and vegetables and how to balance nutrition for wellness.

My parents and grandparents left the soda fountain business in the early 1950s and turned their attention to farming. We grew apples, pears, apricots, peaches, and grapes and had a small patch of strawberries and boysenberries for our personal use. We also had a pomegranate tree and a small almond orchard. Our own cow provided us wonderfully fresh raw milk and cream while chickens and rabbits supplied us with fresh eggs and meat. My grandmother continued her pie-making tradition with the juicy, sweet boysenberries that grew along the fence. She and my mom canned fruit, jams, and tomatoes for our winter enjoyment, and we traded with other farmers for items we didn't can ourselves so that our pantry contained a wide variety of foods. My dad also had a large vegetable garden from which he harvested corn, tomatoes, peppers, green beans, peas, squash, and melons. We enjoyed these fresh during the summer and fall, literally within minutes of picking. We dried some of our apricots, peaches, and grapes. The incredible experience of sitting in a fruit tree, stuffing myself with fruit and letting juices run down my arms and legs is unforgettable. I have been indelibly imprinted with the love of fresh, ripe fruits and vegetables.

These wonderful food experiences and my fledgling cooking skills, which were practiced on my two younger brothers, accompanied me to college, where I sometimes cooked for roommates. However, I was mostly honing my skills as a scientist during the third phase of my culinary journey.

As I concentrated on rows of test tubes instead of rows of vegetables, a remarkable transformation was occurring in grocery stores across the United States. Rows of food burgeoned in the middle aisle, transforming the once small stores that offered fresh, local, and seasonal fruits and vegetables into mega stores. The store layouts of my youth—service meat and fish counters, with one small case of dairy products, single long "coffins" of frozen foods, and an assortment of canned fruits and vegetables—were gone.

In their place sprung supermarkets that offered an ever-increasing assortment of prepared foods, snacks, beverages, and frozen items, including boxed ice cream, which bears little resemblance to the real stuff I grew up enjoying. Meat, poultry, and fish are now prepackaged, and any interaction with the butcher is rare. You can ring a bell and contact a department person for cuts that you don't see in the open case, but the shopper is encouraged to make selections without interacting with anyone. About the only talking you're likely to hear is someone on his or her cell phone.

We now have two generations of Americans who have grown up with little experience of real food, fresh seasonal fruits and vegetables, meat from range-fed animals, unadulterated dairy products, and fresh eggs. Two-income or single-parent households and children who are driven to school and enrolled in a growing number of after-school activities complicate our lives. Fast, easy meals have become the norm, and most families eat out two or three times a week. Supermarkets are meeting customer demand for meals on the go with packaged frozen and refrigerated take-home meals, but the lists of ingredients are unbelievably long and read like a chemistry manual. Along with our love affair with fast food and the expanding middle section of the supermarket has come the expanding middle section of the American body.

We need to get back to the basics of enjoying good fresh food, and I'll show you how to do it. My husband, who shares my history of sitting in peach trees with juice running all over the place, and our three sons were raised with our convergent family philosophies of serving only the finest ingredients prepared at home. However, it was the next step in my culinary travels that has been the basis for my 7-Color Cuisine plan.

My parents rescued me from the scientific world when they bought a health food store in Santa Rosa, California. I pulled my head away from the microscope and test tubes long enough to become intrigued by—but highly skeptical of—the healing benefits of nutrients. What if eating good, fresh food carefully prepared and enjoyed with family and friends could alter the course of cancer, which I was studying at the time? I left the lab and returned to the classroom with a new resolve to find out how the molecules in food might modify body chemistry.

My husband, our sons, and I moved to Santa Rosa to run the family business when my parents retired in 1980. I found my niche showing others how to prepare healthier cuisine. I taught the principles and techniques that I'd developed throughout my life on how to live healthier and overcome various conditions simply by changing attitudes about food. I urged the people in my classes to demand only the freshest, highest-quality ingredients and to cook most meals at home.

Santa Rosa was a wonderful place to do this work because it had a large rural area with local farmers' markets nearly every day of the week. The health food industry was still young, so health food stores were the only place where you could find whole grains, whole-grain products, organic beans and brown rice, healthy oils, unadulterated dairy products, farm-fresh eggs, and local produce. In the minds of most people we were all "health food nuts"! Still, it was a joyous experience to see the faces of others light up when enthusiastically embracing my "new cuisine," which was really just getting back to basics. This was definitely more fun than minding test tubes, even if I was now completely outside the scientific mainstream. Soon I was heading across the country, giving seminars on the health benefits of choosing a more colorful diet and eliminating sugar and additives.

Today, health foods have gained greater acceptance as the demand for organic food and more healthful ingredients has birthed natural food markets such as Whole Foods and Wild Oats. Meanwhile, the importance of diet, particularly whole grains and fresh fruits and vegetables, to disease prevention has now been accepted by mainstream science. Of particular interest to scientists are the natural pigments in these foods that give them their amazing disease-preventing properties.

Natural food markets, with their concentration on fresh organic food, range-fed meats, fresh fish and poultry, take me back to my childhood. They offer an amazing assortment of whole-grain staples and hard-to-find gourmet items that appeal to my sense of adventure in trying new foods. These stores have service meat, poultry, and fish counters where you can get advice on preparing the butcher's selection of the day. Shopping one of these stores lends exciting possibilities for preparing meals with greater taste and appeal. You'll also find take-home entrées, salads, and bakery items made from fresh, whole ingredients minus the chemicals. Upscale markets throughout the country are now offering beautiful produce—some organic—and a wider range of organic and whole-grain staples. Many also offer freshly prepared foods. Even big box stores offer a limited selection of organic staples to meet the needs of a more aware public.

You may not have a natural foods market near you, but there undoubtedly is a local farmers' market where you can buy seasonal produce at incredibly low prices. Many farmers have formed cooperatives through which fresh perishables that may not be available in the immediate area can be sold locally. Farmers' markets are where your new gastronomic adventure using the 7-Color Cuisine plan will begin. I'll lead you through the steps that have helped hundreds of people overcome annoying conditions and enjoy totally new dining experiences. This is a flexible, practical plan that anyone can implement, and you can take it as slowly as needed to get used to unfamiliar foods. As you gain confidence and experience with the plan, you'll want to move on to other 7-Color Cuisine journeys with me.

Acknowledgments

HERE'S TO MY exquisite childhood memories of Rey-Stone's Fountain on the corner of Haight and Clayton Streets in San Francisco. I have special memories of living on our two farms in Watsonville and Modesto, California, sharing with my brothers, Dick and Mike Stone, and my future spouse, Jon Zimmerman, the joy of sweet peach juice running down our arms and all over our clothing.

"Take pleasure in life and enjoy what you eat!" My good friend, Joan Jackson, ends her weekly column in the *Chico Enterprise Record* with this lovely message. Joan has encouraged me to roll up my sleeves and prepare salads for the masses. With her easy-going manner of encouragement I have actually been able to write a book for those not versed in the culinary arts and have a blast doing it!

This book has truly been a journey of love and dedication. My editor, Ginny Ray, graphic designer Jeff Potter, and photographer Karen Sinell have gone to extraordinary lengths to bring this beautiful book to fruition. My friend Arnette Goodman generously lent her beautiful one-of-a-kind pottery pieces for the photos and some of my cooking demonstrations. Patricia Call is one of my closest friends, and together we dashed around Manhattan to assemble the necessary salad ingredients to demonstrate super salad savvy for the masses at the Jacob Javits Convention Center.

—Marcia Rey Stone Zimmerman
December 2006

Introduction

7-COLOR CUISINE™: MAKING HEALTHY, COLORFUL FOODS A LIFESTYLE FOR NUTRITION AND GOOD EATING is for busy people who need to improve their diets but don't know where to begin. Working with the book is like having a personal nutrition coach in your kitchen guiding you to new pleasure in your dining experience. I'll help you unlock the keys to the treasures of good, healthy eating in four simple, easy-to-follow steps. My 7-Color Cuisine system is a complete course in eating for optimum wellness that includes shopping guides, menu plans, recipes and useful tips to make your meals not only feasts for your eyes and treats for your palate, but nourishing for your mind and body.

As a scientist and nutritionist, I've looked at how we eat and what we eat with a clinical eye.

As a meal planner and family chef, I have also looked at how we eat and what we eat with a loving eye.

I know both ways of looking are necessary to making and eating meals, for ourselves and our families, to answer the psychological and physiological needs we bring to every table when we sit down to a meal. And that's why I've developed the 7-Color Cuisine system.

Preparing a meal and enjoying it should be an enjoyable, satisfying culinary experience that engages your senses of smell, vision, and taste. The 7-Color plan guides you through the total experience. It is the perfect antidote for those who have viewed food as the enemy or have never known what it is like to feel fully satisfied by what they've just eaten. What we eat becomes part of us through digestive transformation, something many of us don't want to think about. Yet food can also satisfy our deepest psychological, neurological, and social being—provided we choose a variety of high-quality and colorful foods. That's what I'll help you do with the 7-Color plan and its four easy steps: get set, go shopping, fix meals, and savor your food

Step One: Get Set

Step One prepares you for a new way of eating by carefully examining what you're currently eating and under what conditions. In this step you'll identify dietary pitfalls that you'll need to remove from your refrigerator, freezer, and pantry. I give you lists of alternatives you can substitute for unhealthy foods and then help you make a new shopping list to stock your pantry from suggested replacements and staple items needed for the recipes in the book. The appendixes provide additional information, including resources for specific foods (Appendix D), a checklist of cookware and utensils you'll use (Appendix E), and measurements conversion (Appendix F).

Step Two: Go Shopping

Step Two explains how to restock your pantry and purchase the fresh ingredients needed for the first week's menus. You'll choose foods by their colors, de-emphasizing the type of food you're selecting. This section also includes helpful storage and shopping tips and shows how to clean and store fresh foods to save time in meal preparation.

Step Three: Fix Meals

Most of the dinner recipes in Step Three will take less than 30 minutes to prepare. I'll point out where slow cooking in a crockpot and accelerated preparation using a pressure cooker can conserve preparation time. My weekly meal plans are simple but elegant and offer beautiful food presented to appeal to both the eye and the palate. The menu plans focus on eating 7 colors every day, and I'll show you exactly how to ease into the system by making adjustments as you progress through each step. Preparing your meals at home using the freshest available ingredients is always my goal, and now yours, too

Step Four: Savor Your Food

Step Four shows you how to enjoy your meals, emphasizing every bite with suggestions for controlling portion size and choosing the best menu items when dining out or at home. I'll also suggest ways to reduce the potentially harmful effects of eating unhealthful foods, because sometimes we all do.

Why Choose Foods by Color?

Nature's healing colors abound in fruits, vegetables, whole grains, legumes, and healthy oils. The colors are actually pigments that come from a special class of chemicals known as *phytonutrients*. When you eat foods of a particular color, you access their particular healing powers. Scientists are just now beginning to understand the medicinal impacts of phytonutrients and why eating fruits and vegetables may be our greatest preventive tool against conditions such as cancer, diabetes, obesity, and heart disease. For many centuries traditional healers have taught color-coded eating as essential for maintaining health, vitality, and long life. From this foundation in traditional medicine and modern scientific investigation, 7-Color Cuisine has emerged.

Eat 7 Colors a Day

The five bright fruit and vegetable colors of red, orange, yellow, green, blue-violet-purple, plus the tan earth tones of grains and legumes, reveal the phytonutrient pedigrees of those foods. Animal foods, including dairy, eggs, fish, and poultry, are creamy white in color and contain healing nutrients called *zoonutrients*. *7-Color Cuisine: Making Healthy, Colorful Foods a Lifestyle for Nutrition and Good Eating* guides you to select foods based on their colors, which yield an array of phytonutrients and zoonutrients that research shows may help fight disease, help you lose weight, derail the aging process, and sharpen your wits. The cookbook integrates planning, buying, storing, and preparing brightly colored foods that heal. And the 7-Color system aims to heighten your awareness of how delicious and satisfying well-prepared good food really can be.

Most nutrition and diet regimens emphasize the composition of food, enumerating how many calories a particular food or recipe contains and its carbohydrate, fat, fiber, and protein content. Although these numbers are important and are included with every recipe in this cookbook, the emphasis in the 7-Color system is on eating the right foods and enjoying them. By unlocking the keys to the 7-Color plan, you'll accomplish your dietary goals without having to play the numbers game.

The plan begins with basics on how phytonutrients protect you and why brightly colored foods are the best food choices to help you look and feel your best. Each color has its own category of protective phytonutrients, and the health benefits of each category are fully explained. Foods making up the category are listed as top picks, and you are encouraged to eat as many different selections as possible. The amount of each color you should eat is also given in detailed, thirty-day meal plans, shopping tips, and recipes for both warm and cool weather. You'll also find a pantry management section to help you track staples and eliminate high-calorie and less-nutritious items. Once you learn the 7-Color plan, you'll be able to mix and match recipes for an endless variety of delicious meals.

Eat Less, Maintain Optimal Weight, and Feel Better

7-Color Cuisine features foods that are fresh and seasonal. They're also nutrient-dense, meaning that they come packaged as nature intended, with hundreds of different beneficial nutrients. Nothing has been removed or processed out of these foods, so they retain natural digestive enzymes, which can help maintain an optimum body balance of acid and alkaline (pH). Learning which foods to avoid and why their consumption can sabotage weight loss and accelerate aging, you'll also feel more satisfied and less inclined to snack. With this system, followers have reported drastic improvements to digestive problems, bloating, and water retention. Many say they have great success maintaining optimal weight and that such maladies as aching joints, skin problems, fatigue, low sex drive, and reduced cognitive function have improved.

This plan is high in protein, much of it from vegetables and legumes, and naturally low in processed carbohydrates and saturated fat, because the emphasis is on vegetables, fruits, whole grains, legumes, lean protein, and healthy oils. As we grow older, we need more protein-rich foods to meet the body's maintenance and repair needs. We also need to choose friendly oils rather than saturated fats to maintain normal cellular and brain function. The 7-Color plan is so easy to follow that you don't have to wonder about how to implement a healthier dietary regimen. It *is* a healthier regime, although it doesn't feel like one. And yet the plan will be unique to you because you will be learning a system that you can adjust to meet your personal goals.

All of the menus and recipes here have been analyzed carefully to make sure they adhere to the latest nutrition recommendations and dietary guidelines. My plan is based on and supported by the latest scientific findings, not the latest food fads. I know the sound nutritional information contained in *7-Color Cuisine: Making Healthy, Colorful Foods a Lifestyle for Nutrition and Good Eating* will endure for a lifetime of more enjoyable and nutritious meals.

Creating Colorful Cuisine

CHAPTER ONE

Guiding Principles

Learning from Nature

Today's fast-paced lifestyle has robbed us of the time we need to care for the most basic human need: sustaining life by feeding ourselves well. We eat more than enough calories, but the quality of what we eat is so poor that it doesn't sustain optimum health. The grab-and-feed mentality of the twenty-first century has obliterated the once-important practice of providing healthy family meals, and we are paying a heavy price. More than half the adult population and a growing number of children are classified as obese, and poor diet is implicated in all chronic diseases. As a culture, we're desperately searching for ways to combat the trend, but we most often look in the wrong places and toward extreme diets and pills.

The plan presented in this book is really simple: Just consider that everything you put into your mouth becomes part of you.

If you are not energized by the color of the food you're eating, that's a clue that it will wind up as fat around your abdomen, waist, thighs, and buttocks. And you may not have the right stuff to think clearly and to combat stress. Do you make a habit of eating on the run? If so, you may be plagued with digestive problems and be less able to access food nutrients.

It's also extremely likely that you will not have the quality of life you hope for as you get older.

My choice, and I hope yours, is to travel along a different path to eating better with the fresh and colorful foods provided by nature.

7-Color Cuisine: Healing the Mind and Body

In the mid-1970s Dr. Stephen DeFelice first used the term *nutraceutical* to describe a broad class of nutrients with disease-fighting properties. Since that time this category has been further defined to highlight important disease-fighting chemicals found in plant and animal foods.

Phytonutrients give plants their bright colors, and we access their healing powers when we eat those brightly colored foods. Animals that eat phytonutrient-rich foods transform them into zoonutrients that color egg yolks and make butter appear yellow and make salmon and trout pink. Range-fed animals and wild game eat phytonutrient grasses and, as a result, their meat contains higher levels of healthy omega-3 fatty acids and conjugated linoleic acid than does that of their grain-fed counterparts. Range animals are also leaner and, if organically raised, their meat doesn't contain hormones or antibiotic residues.

Over the last century, changes in the way animals are fed, shifting from range-fed to feed, has led to substantial change in meat quality. If you're a big meat-eater, it's even more important that you get your daily servings of vegetables and fruits to balance the potential health challenges presented by a diet rich in meat. Eating the right colors every day is the basis of my new system, but other factors play into it for a full and satisfying culinary experience, including mindfulness, shopping without distraction, and preparing meals with intention.

The Need for Mindfulness

The 7-Color system emphasizes the need to be fully engaged in what you're doing, whether you're shopping, cooking, or eating. Set aside multitasking and enjoy cooking to its fullest. Get to know the deep satisfaction in shopping for the most colorful foods and planning menus around them to nourish your whole person as one of your greatest weapons against stress.

As we grow older, mindfulness becomes more important. One definition of aging includes a decline in our ability to cope with environmental, psychological, and physiological stresses. As our adaptive ability decreases, our immune systems are less able to respond appropriately to challenges, leading to an increased tendency toward illness. By keeping your mind fully engaged in the current moment, you may be able to reduce stress and mitigate the chance of developing chronic conditions.

Shopping Without Distraction

When you shop, do so with as little distraction as possible so that you have time to read labels and think about what you're buying. Plan two or three shopping times per week, including during the weekend and midweek. These trips can be short stops at the produce, fish, and dairy sections, because you will have already established and maintained your dry pantry of staple goods. Make shopping times a priority by scheduling them as weekly events. And be sure to take a shopping list and avoid browsing in supermarkets, because if you don't, you're much more likely to buy items with clever marketing and packaging that hide less healthful qualities.

Before heading to the store, review your menu plans and list the items you'll need for the suggested menus. (Worksheets are included in Appendix C to help you figure that out as an on-going task). As you become more adept at working with the 7-Color system, you'll get used to selecting the choicest fruits and vegetables and be able to pair them quickly with grains, legumes, and animal source foods to build your own color-based menus. Using the menu plans, you'll also have an endless array of combinations to choose from.

To keep your pantry well stocked, you'll maintain a running list of needed items in a convenient location, perhaps on the refrigerator. If you've noted specifics, you'll see when particular shelf pantry items are running low, as you will with staples that you always want to have on hand in the refrigerator. You'll want to update your list as you prepare meals to replenish any ingredients used. (Complete lists of wet and dry staples can be found in Appendix C).

Preparing Meals with Intention

You'll find daily menu plans with recipes and list of ingredients to buy in Part Two. With a purposeful plan for meal preparation, the first step is to establish your food preparation area and remove all nonessential items. That's important whether your kitchen is small or large. Arrange the items you use most in a drawer adjacent to the food preparation area. Make sure that the area is clean and, as you work, use a damp bar towel to wipe your hands and clean spills fast.

Rinse the bar towel frequently and change it daily. If you make clean-up a part of food preparation, you'll eliminate the unpleasant task of returning to a disaster (when everyone is relaxed) after a great meal.

Reserve one chopping board for raw fish, poultry, and meat and scrub it thoroughly with detergent after each use. Other boards used for vegetables need only to be cleaned with water.

Assemble all of the ingredients, cookware, and utensils you need to prepare a recipe. Small items like fresh herbs, onions, and garlic can be chopped and set aside in small bowls until you're ready to use them. (There's a list of essential equipment and gadgets in Appendix D.)

While you're preparing the meal, someone who's going to eat it might well help you by setting an attractive table. Many working couples use the tag-team idea, and that's much more fun than working alone, plus it allows you to release the workday mind-set.

If you eat your meals alone it's even more important for you to "stage" your dining area with an attractive place setting and soft music or whatever helps you relax. Candlelight sets a wonderful mood for dining anytime. A candle flame's intense energy can serve to remind you of the renewed energy your food will provide and help you focus on what you are eating.

Parents can get children involved with meal preparation and make it a time for informal conversation and discussion about proper nutrition. Traditionally the kitchen has been the hub of the home where family and friends gather during meal preparation. People are drawn to the sight and smell of good food being well prepared, and that warm feeling also helps stimulate good digestion. When the mind is fully engaged in food preparation, signals are sent from the brain to the digestive organs, allowing them to produce the right blend of acids and enzymes to digest the meal's contents.

Enjoying Your Meal

Enjoy what you are eating and take your time. Think about how wonderful each bite tastes and how it will nourish your body. You'll rediscover that one of life's greatest pleasures is enjoying good food. By eating slowly and thoughtfully you'll feel full eating smaller portions. Keep out as much distraction as possible and carry on a pleasant conversation with those you love. A meal is not the proper time to settle arguments or rebuke family members for misdeeds. It's better to listen to music than to watch television during dinner because television is too distracting and often deeply disturbing.

People who dine alone often like to read while they eat. And that's fine as long as you make sure to enjoy every bite and stop frequently to savor the sweetness of good food. And do read something pleasant and uplifting. If your work involves travel, you'll have to devise some special strategies to eat 7 colors each day while on the road and enjoy what you eat. Al, for example, travels 50 percent of his time, and he finds that reading something inspirational during breakfast helps him focus later on his high-tech presentations. He selects fresh fruit and either a vegetable omelet or old-fashioned oatmeal with yogurt, depending on his plans for the day. If he's taking clients to lunch, then breakfast and dinner will be lighter meals. Al keeps mealtime with his clients low-key, focusing on enjoying their company and exploring common interests rather than promoting his products and services.

Most of us eat too much food and never feel quite satisfied. On a trip to Dallas I booked a room in a hotel that was hosting a convention for a group called "Take Off Pounds Sensibly" or "TOPS." While visiting with a woman at the breakfast counter one morning, I pushed my half-full plate away. She was amazed that I could be full and told that she had never known what that felt like. Later you'll read about some of my clients and how they overcame the feeling of never being full when they followed the 7-Color system. You will eat less yet feel more satisfied. The trick is to choose the right foods and keep portion size under control.

The Importance of Presentation

Adults age fifty and older and those who wish to lose weight should serve their main courses on nine-inch salad plates. To enhance the meal's presentation and make it more visually appealing, place the food in the middle of the plate and garnish it with a sprig of fresh herbs or colorful strips of raw vegetables. A plate heaping with food and spilling over the sides is really unappealing, except maybe at Thanksgiving, a holiday that celebrates food with great conviviality.

It's best to serve main course accompaniments like salads on seven-inch bread-and-butter plates. Use small bowls to hold dipping sauce, brown rice, or vegetables. Serving various courses on separate plates heightens the intrigue and encourages mindfulness as you choose which plate to sample from next. Children know this innately. They hate it when the gravy runs all over the vegetables, and many find it disgusting if different types of food even touch one another.

The recipes here are planned for two people who are either on a weight-loss regimen or in their middle or later years, but they can be scaled easily to feed a bigger crowd at the table.

CHAPTER TWO

Savor the Sweetness of Good, Colorful Food

The Slow Food Movement

The enjoyment of good food, particularly in the company of like-minded people, is the goal of the worldwide slow food movement. Founded in 1986 by Italy's Carlo Petrini in response to the opening of the first McDonald's in Rome, the slow food movement recognizes the vital relationship between ecology and gastronomy. It seeks to counter the annihilation of traditional food varieties and the proliferation of fast foods by offering a greater number of food choices and by supporting sustainable agriculture, the purity of organic foods, and a greater appreciation for social and cultural food traditions. Currently there are 80,000 members in fifty countries.

Slow Food USA, with 140 chapters and 12,000 members, espouses better lifestyles by celebrating food bio-diversity, encouraging slower food preparation, and celebrating meals with convivial companions. The organization aims to honor generations of families who have been committed to sustainable agriculture and bio-diversity of plant and animal species and their devotion to processes that yield the greatest taste sensations. That happens when we preserve heritage fruits and vegetables, maintain diverse animal and poultry lines, and make our own beer, wine, farmhouse-style cheeses, and other artisan products. The goals of the slow food movement align well with the 7-Color Cuisine plan, which depends on the availability of fresh, seasonal foods from small local farms found everywhere in the country. The slow food movement naturally provides balanced nutritional support through the selection and quality of food that it promotes.

Acid–Alkaline Balance

The human body maintains an optimal pH of 7.4, and even a slight shift up or down has a dramatic effect on metabolism. To ensure optimum pH, the body has developed an efficient buffering system using agents derived from food and water. Fruits and vegetables range in their inherent pH factors, but it is the alkalizing minerals they contain that buffer acids in animal foods, grains, and beans. People who eat primarily animal source foods, and highly processed foods or those laden with sugar and fat, are in chronic acidosis because they're not getting the alkaline-buffering minerals in fruits and vegetables.

With its emphasis on fruits and vegetables, the 7-Color plan can reduce many of the unpleasant symptoms encountered by those with acidic systems. They include fatigue, loss of motivation, irritability, nervousness, insomnia, headaches, gastric distress, bowel problems, rectal burning, edema, runny nose, sinusitis, chronic colds, thin brittle nails, leg cramps, muscle spasms, joint pain, stiff neck, poor circulation, and various forms of inflammation or infection.

Dietary Challenges to pH Balance

One of the most acidifying and potentially harmful things humans can do is regularly consume soft drinks. According to the December 2000 edition of the *International Journal of Integrative Medicine*, one 12-ounce can of cola (pH 2.8 to 3.2) must be diluted one-hundred-fold to change the pH to 5, the lowest pH for liquids that the kidneys can safely excrete. But doing so would produce an additional 33 liters of urine—certainly capturing most people's attention.

Instead the body balances the beverage's low pH with minerals from foods. And if those minerals aren't available, the body draws them from tissue to neutralize the phosphoric acid and sweetener in the beverage. Sodium and potassium are pulled from tissues first; if those reserves are too low, then the body buffers the acid influx by pulling calcium, magnesium, and other minerals from bones. This subtle process is not noticed as it's happening, but after doing it for years, the body may pay a heavy price.

Frequent consumption of soda also causes significant mineral loss that can lead to periodontal problems, muscle cramping, bone thinning, and osteoporosis. We tend to think these conditions occur only in older people, but the high consumption of soda among teenagers, who are developing peak bone mass during those years, poses a great risk for higher rates of bone thinning, fracture, and osteoporosis later.

Stress and excessive exercise also increase acidity in the body. The 7-Color plan shows how our attitudes about food and the ways we prepare and enjoy our meals can help lower stress. Mindfulness is the most important step we can take to control it. In addition, those who exercise intensely need to be particularly careful to eat diets high in fruits and vegetables so that protein comes primarily from vegetable sources. The plan provides a significant percentage of alkaline foods with acid-buffering properties.

Raw Versus Cooked Foods

There's growing consensus among health experts that eating more raw fruits and vegetables is healthier than eating fewer. Whole, "live" foods contain the highest nutrient levels and essential metabolic and digestive enzymes needed to digest and utilize the food we eat. Raw foods, especially papayas, pineapples, and garlic, contain varying amounts of enzymes.

These enzymes, which are destroyed by high heat, take over much of the digestive process, transforming minerals into the alkaline buffers needed to counteract today's highly acidic diet. Foods that have been processed and otherwise altered from their natural state become more acidic and less nourishing. Processing also strips the life out of food. David Wolfe, an expert on raw food nutrition and founder of Nature's First Law, listed the three most important things we should know about raw foods: life force, enzymes, and conservation of resources (also known as sustainability).

Raw foods contain a life force that permits sprouting and growth; we can see this in raw vegetables that grow in a refrigerator where carrots sprout new tops, and potatoes grow new buds. Cooked vegetables not only do not grow, but also decay as fungi, molds, and bacteria decompose them. The less foods are cooked and the more life force that remains in them, the more resistant those foods are to decay. Raw foods also have the plus of containing significant amounts of water, providing a clean source of this vital fluid.

Eating natural, raw food is also more ecologically efficient. Raw foods are naturally "prepackaged" with all the nutrients needed for human growth and so take less of the Earth's resources to provide food for its people. Another important health factor is how much and how many environmental contaminants are contained in foods. These contaminants become concentrated each step up the food chain. Eating plant foods, which are at the bottom, means adding less toxicity to our bodies. Animals retain ten times more contaminants than do the plants they eat, so when we eat animal meat, contaminants are concentrated one-hundred-fold.

In addition to vitamins, minerals, and enzymes, many raw foods contain chlorophyll, considered by leading herbalists to be a good detoxifying and cleansing agent. Finally, raw foods are excellent alkalizing agents. Green foods are alkalizing and boost tissue oxygenation. That's why chlorophyll-rich foods are included in most cleansing and detoxifying programs.

Despite the many advantages of raw foods, humans have long used various forms of food processing to "cook" their foods, varying the process by climate and culture. People have boiled, baked, fried, fermented, pickled, smoked, cultured, juiced, chopped, sprouted, salted, dried, milled, canned, and frozen food for eons. And there are advantages in using these methods to make food more digestible. Today light cooking helps tame a pile of raw greens that would otherwise be too intimidating. For example, a pound of raw spinach can be lightly steamed so that it wilts to just two cups. It retains its appealing, bright green color and nutrients but yields its water. Light steaming also removes oxalic acid from spinach, kale, and other dark green vegetables that binds food minerals and makes them unavailable to the body. In the 7-Color plan, food preparation becomes a mental as well as a physical exercise, helping reduce stress and improve digestion in numerous ways.

Whether we choose menus with cold or warm foods depends on the season, the climate, and an innate sense of what our bodies need. (Several excellent soup recipes for cold weather are included in this text; soups are one of the most nourishing ways to combine foods with diverse nutritional benefits.) The 7-Color plan provides a balance between raw and cooked foods that's satisfying and nourishing for all body types. All you have to do is tune in to your body's response and choose and lovingly prepare fresh, organic foods that can be enjoyed with like-minded companions.

Why Organic Foods Are Better

Nutritional Drawbacks to Chemicals and Pesticides
Scientists have found that the increasing use of chemicals and pesticides to grow "better" food since World War II has dramatically reduced the mineral content of commercially grown fruits and vegetables. Overall calcium levels have been reduced by 29 percent, magnesium by 21 percent, potassium by 6 percent, and iron by 32 percent. Pesticides and herbicides also appear to thwart the production of phenolics, phytonutrients that are natural plant defenses and are included among some of the most important antioxidants for optimum human health.

Pesticides and herbicides also leave residue on fruits and vegetables that's toxic to us. The U.S. Department of Agriculture (USDA), for instance, routinely analyzes for more than 150 chemical residues in poultry and meat and recently found that one day's intake of conventional foods (three meals and two snacks) included thirty-seven potential toxins.

Nutritional Advantages of Organic Foods

Organic food is raised and processed without the use of persistent synthetic pesticides, artificial ingredients, or preservatives. Organic farmers don't use radiation or genetically modified organisms in food production, instead they rely on natural composts and manure to renew soil and rotate crops to prevent the depletion of vital nutrients. The result is food with significantly more vitamin C, iron, magnesium, and phosphorus than conventional food and fewer harmful nitrates and heavy metals. The protein content of organic crops has been found to be lower, but of better quality, translating directly into greater health benefits.

Small differences in nutrient content add up over time. Eating five servings of organic fruits and vegetables each day, for example, provides the recommended daily intake of vitamin C, essential for optimal resistance to infection and the maintenance of connective tissue. The same number of servings of commercial produce, however, would not provide even the minimum daily intake. Low vitamin C intake may present significant health risks of various types, as evidenced in one study that found sperm counts in men who ate organic foods were much higher than those in men who ate conventional produce.

By following the guidelines in *7-Color Cuisine* to buy local organic produce in season, you'll be sure to get the highest nutrient content possible in the food you eat. For example, the USDA database states that fresh, red tomatoes purchased in season (from June through October) contain more than twice the vitamin C than those bought out of season (from November through May). And scientists at Rutgers University who set out to disprove the claim that "organic is better" were astounded to find that organic spinach contained 97 percent more iron and 99 percent more manganese than samples of conventionally produced spinach. In addition, many essential trace minerals were completely absent in the commercial produce, but relatively abundant in their organically grown counterparts.

The Health Benefits of Organic Foods

Organic food is now the fastest-growing sector of U.S. agriculture. According to a 2003 CNN report, organic food sales were expected to reach $13 billion by year's end. Why all the interest in organic foods? The Organic Trade Association, based in Greenfield, Massachusetts, lists ten good reasons to go organic on its Web site. Comments relate each reason to enjoy 7-Color Cuisine:

- Organic food tastes great; better taste sensations come from strong, healthy, unadulterated food.
- Organic production reduces health risks, particularly to agricultural workers who otherwise handle the poisons used to make prettier plants, but also to consumers who are exposed daily to an ever-growing list of potentially harmful chemicals in conventionally produced fruit and vegetables.
- Organic farms respect water resources; they reduce the pollution and contamination of waterways caused by nitrate fertilizer filtration through the soil.
- Organic farmers build healthy soil by composting and through crop rotation.
- Organic farmers work in harmony with nature by using natural insect predators and weed-control methods and by preserving wetlands and other natural resources, the practice of which is more labor-intensive.

- Organic producers are leaders in innovative research to reduce dependence on pesticides and the potential negative effects of agriculture on the environment.
- Organic producers preserve bio-diversity by growing a wider variety of species.
- Organic farming helps keep rural communities healthy in a time when small family farms struggle against large conventional farms.
- Organic abundance: Clothing and other goods, in addition to food, are increasingly available.

The Price of Organic Foods

Organic produce is increasingly the choice of consumers who want superior flavor, color, and nutrient content in the food they eat, but it does cost a little more at the register. Many people are willing to pay extra for the benefit of eating food that hasn't been sprayed with chemicals or grown with synthetic fertilizers, but some shoppers remain deterred by the price.

What isn't apparent at the seemingly lower tally for conventional food at the register is that those shoppers are actually paying three times. First, they pay at the register. Second, their tax dollars subsidize conventional farmers, but not organic farmers. Third, consumers are paying for cleaning up the environment and for untold health costs that result from the environmental pollution due to conventional farming, production, and packaging methods. If these hidden factors were added to the cost of conventional food, then organic foods would cost the same or perhaps even less. It's encouraging to know that despite paying more at the register, consumers are becoming more aware of the benefits of organically grown products and opting for organic choices in food and other commodities.

7-Color Cuisine and the New Food Guide Pyramid

In April 2005 the USDA unveiled its new Food Guide Pyramid. The new guide features colored food groupings, which is a step in the right direction. And, for the first time, the guide emphasizes exercise and smaller portion size. But the guide's suggestion that there are really twelve different pyramids and that each of us needs a specific one unnecessarily complicates the pyramid. (Visit the USDA Web site [www.mypyramid.gov] to find your personal pyramid.) Margo Wootan, nutrition policy director for the Center for Science in the Public Interest in Washington, D.C., sees the over-complication. "There are simple, key principles about healthy eating that truly do work for all Americans, and those could have been represented on one symbol," she writes. "USDA really dodged the politically difficult message of encouraging Americans to eat less."

The USDA also missed the point of choosing foods by color in failing to categorize them according to the actual colors we see when shopping,. This makes it more difficult for us to remember and apply the guidelines. For example, the pyramid represents dairy products as blue. The 7-Color plan refers to dairy products as creamy white, their actual color. 7-Color Cuisine does adhere to the new dietary guidelines by emphasizing fruits and vegetables, whole grains, and fewer fatty and sugar-laden foods.

CHAPTER THREE

The 7-Color Cuisine Plan

ACH COLOR IN the 7-Color Cuisine plan is important because it offers a unique kind of potential protection against aging and disease. The amount of each color that should be consumed each day is indicated by its size in the pie chart in Figure 3-1 (color plate after page 30).

Phytonutrients have a synergistic effect, and that's why all 7 colors should be eaten every day. Weill Medical College's September 2001 newsletter, *Food and Fitness Advisor*, recently reported that the cancer-fighting power of foods is greater when different-colored foods are consumed at the same meal (such as broccoli with tomatoes) than when eaten alone. The 7-Color plan offers a rainbow of foods with loads of naturally occurring, disease-fighting phytonutrients and zoonutrients. In planning daily menus, we've accounted for the correct amounts of each color of food. With a little practice, you'll soon become adept at planning your own menus using this color wheel.

The idea that the color of food determines its effect on the body originated long ago. Taoist philosophy dating back thousands of years uses the colors of food to define them as *yin* or *yang*. Plant foods, particularly those of purple and violet hues, are soft and cooling (yin) and the best choices during warm weather. Summer provides a bounty of deep purple and violet berries, figs, grapes, and plums. Animal foods are considered hard and warming (yang). Warm reds and oranges are also yang. We naturally crave more meat, legumes, and warm, starchy foods such as carrots, squash, and yams in cold weather. Neutral green and yellow foods help provide a good balance during any season. The 7-Color plan provides balanced eating throughout the year.

Eating Seven Colors Every Day

By following the 7-Color plan, you'll eat ½ cup of red, orange, yellow, and purple foods, choosing from a variety of fruits and vegetables. In addition, you'll choose 2 cups of fruits or green vegetables or both, including salad greens, and 2 cups of cereal, brown rice, pasta, whole-grain breads, beans, and a few nuts or seeds. You can make up your own plan combining the daily amounts of one or two colors in a single meal.

The important difference in 7-Color planning is its emphasis on creating meals around the most colorful foods and adding animal foods as you prefer: 8 ounces of fish, poultry, eggs, legumes, or meat; and 2 cups of dairy or soy products; plus healthy oils and condiments. This is opposite to what most of us are accustomed to thinking when planning meals. Americans think first of meat, then add vegetables and fruit as an afterthought. Healthy snacks can also be colorful and a great way to fit in servings of fruit and vegetables.

It's important for you to follow the 7-Color menu plans as closely as possible right from the beginning because colorful meals are more appealing and tasty as well as nutritious. But the plan isn't meant to be rigid; if you miss your purple food one day, then make sure to eat it the next Take a break on weekends, if you like, but stay with the plan during the week. If 7-Color Cuisine departs radically from the way you're used to eating, then work into it slowly. Start, for example, by mixing darker green lettuce (more nutritious) with iceberg lettuce in salads, or mix brown rice with white. If you like pasta, try the colorful vegetable pastas first and then whole-wheat pasta. Remember that it's rather uncomfortable for anyone to have a nutrition fanatic as a dining partner, so take it easy and respect the food preferences of others.

Here's an example of how the plan works.

BREAKFAST

+ ½ cup blueberries
+ ¾ cup granola
+ ½ cup yogurt, plain, low-fat
+ 1 teaspoon ground cinnamon
+ 6-ounce glass tomato or cranberry juice

NUTRITION FACTS	
calories	395
fat	3.9 grams
saturated fat	0.5 grams
cholesterol	2 milligrams
sodium	346 milligrams
carbohydrate	76.1 grams
fiber	7.2 grams
protein	14 grams

LUNCH

+ 1½ cups leek and potato soup (left over from the previous evening's dinner)
+ rainbow fruit and nut with pomegranate blueberry vinaigrette

DINNER FOR TWO

+ Stir fry vegetable medley
+ Steamed salmon topped with fresh tarragon and lemon
+ Brown rice and wild rice combo

Leek and Potato Soup

NUTRITION FACTS

calories	183
fat	8.2 grams
saturated fat	1.6 grams
cholesterol	4 milligrams
sodium	264 milligrams
carbohydrate	22.9 grams
fiber	2 grams
protein	4.3 grams

Add 1 tablespoon low-fat yogurt or fat-free sour cream to each serving.

INGREDIENTS

2 large leeks, washed, chopped, green tops removed

2 tablespoons organic extra virgin olive oil

½ cup cilantro leaves, chopped

1 large potato, peeled and chopped

1 quart fat-free chicken stock

Freshly ground black pepper

1 cup 2% fat milk

1 rounded tablespoon arrowroot powder

Low-fat yogurt or fat-free sour cream (1 tablespoon per serving)

DIRECTIONS

1. In a 3½-quart pressure cooker or pot, sauté leeks in organic olive oil over medium heat. Add cilantro, potato, chicken stock, and pepper.

2. Cook 15 minutes at 8 pounds per square inch (psi) in a pressure cooker (use natural release method) or in a covered pot for 45 minutes.

3. Let cool slightly and process 2 cups at a time in a blender or food processor. Return to the pressure cooker or pot.

4. Add low-fat milk to blender and blend in arrowroot powder. Add mixture to soup and stir frequently until soup just comes to a boil. Turn off heat.

Super Salad—Rainbow Fruit and Nut with Pomegranate Blueberry Vinaigrette

NUTRITION FACTS

calories	164
fat	0 grams
saturated fat	0 grams
cholesterol	0 milligrams
sodium	85 milligrams
carbohydrate	33 grams
fiber	5.3 grams
protein	3.3 grams

INGREDIENTS PER PERSON

2 cups baby spring greens or arugula

½ cup peeled and sliced orange halves, 3 slices

½ cup sliced red or yellow apple halves, 3 slices

1 tablespoon dry roasted macadamia nuts, no salt added

1 tablespoon dried cranberries

1 tablespoon pomegranate blueberry vinaigrette

DIRECTIONS

Assemble following Super Salad Savvy plan.

Steamed Salmon with Tarragon and Lemon

NUTRITION FACTS

calories	362
fat	13.2 grams
saturated fat	2.7 grams
cholesterol	97 milligrams
sodium	94 milligrams
carbohydrates	12.5 grams
fiber	5.2 grams
protein	48.2 grams

NOTE: *Top each salmon steak with ½ tablespoon fresh chopped tarragon and serve with fresh lemon wedges.*

NOTE: *If desired, add 1 tea-spoon of tartar sauce per serving of salmon. Add the nutrition information from the bottle to the nutrition facts given above.*

INGREDIENTS

- **2 salmon steaks or fillets (2 portions, 6 ounces each)**
- **2 large, fresh tarragon branches with leaves**
- **1 tablespoon tarragon leaves, chopped for garnish**
- **1 sliced lemon**
- **1 quartered lemon**
- **Tartar sauce, optional**

DIRECTIONS

1. Wash and pat salmon dry.

2. Place in one section of a steamer and cover with tarragon branches and lemon slices.

3. Steam for approximately 20 minutes until fish flakes but no raw, pink flesh remains.

4. Remove and discard tarragon and lemon.

Brown and Wild Rice with Mushrooms

NUTRITION FACTS

calories 183
fat 1.4 grams
saturated fat 0.3 grams
cholesterol 0 milligrams
sodium 180 milligrams
carbohydrates 38 grams
fiber 2 grams
protein 4.6 grams

This makes enough rice for leftovers.

INGREDIENTS

- **1 cup dry, organic mixed brown-and-wild-rice blend**
- **1 cup chopped mushrooms**
- **2 cups fat-free chicken broth or 2 cups water with 1 teaspoon dissolved fat-free chicken soup base**

DIRECTIONS

1. Place the ingredients in the rice-cooking compartment of a steamer.
2. Cover and steam for 45 to 55 minutes or until all liquid has been absorbed and rice is tender.
3. Alternative: Place ingredients in a pressure cooker and process for 22 to 25 minutes at 8 psi. Use the natural release method.

Stir Fry Vegetable Medley

NUTRITION FACTS

calories	73
fat	3.7 grams
saturated fat	0.5 grams
cholesterol	0 milligrams
sodium	17 milligrams
carbohydrates	8.9 grams
fiber	2.9 grams
protein	1.2 grams

NOTE: *You can add 1 cup fresh tomatoes or 1 large roasted red bell pepper if you have another color juice for breakfast*

INGREDIENTS

- **1 cup yellow crookneck squash, cut into bite-sized pieces**
- **1 cup carrots, cut into strips**
- **1 cup chopped green peppers**
- **½ cup sliced shallots**
- **1 tablespoon extra virgin organic olive oil**
- **¼ cup chopped parsley or other green herb such as basil, oregano, or cilantro**
- **Freshly ground black pepper**

DIRECTIONS

In a large wok, lightly sauté chopped vegetables until tender. Add chopped parsley or other green herb and pepper.

Red	tomato or cranberry juice, cinnamon
Orange	mandarins, carrots in soup
Yellow	vegetable medley
Purple	blueberries, purple lettuce in mesclun
Green	Super Salad, soup, and vegetable medley
Tan	granola, brown-and-wild-rice combo
White	yogurt, salmon, goat cheese

Count Colors—
Be Nutritionally Correct

This daily menu is a template for the thirty-day menu plans you'll find in Chapter Six. Count colors—not calories—and you'll be nutritionally correct! Let's see how this works.

Count Calories and Nutrients

A quick glance at the values shows that the 7-Color plan is low in fat, saturated fat, cholesterol, and sodium—all with the goal of improving your health. The plan is also high in fiber and protein while lower in complex carbohydrates than standard recommended values. That's because 7-Color Cuisine is geared for those who want antiaging effects or to lose weight. The basic plan as presented here is perfect for those older than fifty who need fewer calories and higher protein, ideally from vegetable sources, than their younger counterparts.

In the thirty daily menu plans you will, however, see that we've also provided for those who require more calories without changing the ratios of colors or nutrition values. There's also room in this plan to add two or three small snacks of fresh fruit, dried fruit, vegetables, or nuts and remain within the recommended daily intake for all nutrients.

Tips for Meal Preparation

If you clean vegetables ahead of time, they'll be ready for quick chopping, reducing preparation time. If you use a steamer to cook the rice, then you can put the salmon in a second compartment during the last half of cooking. The rice recipe makes approximately 3 cups; a serving size is 1 cup per person. You can use the extra rice for a tasty lunch, especially if you add a few more vegetables to the medley and reserve the extra vegetables to enjoy with the rice. I'm a big fan of bottled, roasted sweet peppers, and I add them to vegetable dishes, omelets, and fish. The peppers taste great, and they are an attractive red.

Nutrition Facts

	Breakfast	Lunch	Dinner	Daily Total	% Daily Total of calories	Daily Recommended Value (DRI)
Calories	395	448	618	1461	*	1500 calories
Total Fat, grams	3.9	20.8	18.3	43	26.5	48.75
Saturated Fat, grams	0.5	9.8	3.5	13.8	8.5	15
Cholesterol, milligrams	2	30	97	129	*	225
Sodium, milligrams	346	480	291	1117	*	1,800
Carbohydrates, grams	76.1	47.8	59.4	183.3	50.2	225
Fiber, grams	7.2	7.6	10.1	24.9	*	18.75
Protein, grams	14	17.3	54	85.3	23.4	37.5

*Does not apply.

The Health Benefits
of Each Color

Red

Red, orange, yellow, and green foods contain *carotenoids*, powerful antioxidants that protect the eyes, skin, and internal organs. *Lycopene*, the red pigment found in tomatoes, watermelon, red peppers, and pink grapefruit, is one of the best known. In fact, lycopene is the most prevalent carotenoid in the circulatory system and has been found to reduce the risk of prostate and other cancers. Another red carotenoid, *astaxanthin*, gives salmon and trout pink color. Although these fish are pink, they receive high ratings among physicians, primarily because they contain healthy omega-3 fats.

Top Picks for Reds

Vegetables (½ cup = 1 serving)	
radishes	red onions
red peppers (sweet and chili)	red-skinned potatoes
tomatoes	
Fruit (½ cup = 1 serving)	
cherries	cranberries
pink grapefruit	pomegranates
red apples	red grapes
red pears	red plums
rhubarb	strawberries
watermelon	
Spices (1 teaspoon powdered)	
allspice	chili powder
cinnamon	cloves
red peppers	

NOTE: *Spices are crucial because they add taste and nutritional value and reduce the need for salt. They don't take the place of vegetables and fruits, but rather enhance their enjoyment. Red foods, except tomatoes, are alkaline buffers.*

SERVINGS PER DAY · Choose one serving (½ cup) of red fruit and vegetables every day. (Red spices contain important antioxidants, too.)

Orange

Beta carotene is the most frequently studied orange carotenoid. Orange-colored foods, such as carrots, apricots, and cantaloupe, contain high levels. Green fruits and vegetables, like green peas and broccoli, are also good sources. But chlorophyll is more intensely colored and hides the carotenes. The deep orange color of winter vegetables, including squash, yams, and pumpkin, indicates their high levels and provides extra protection against cold weather conditions. Winter vegetables are loaded with complex carbohydrates, excellent sources of extra energy to help keep you warm. The body converts beta carotene to vitamin A, an immune system protector. Serve an extra helping of these starchy vegetables in-

Top Picks for Orange

Vegetables (½ cup = 1 serving)	
carrots	orange peppers
pumpkins	sweet potatoes
winter squash	yams
Fruit (½ cup = 1 serving)	
apricots	cantaloupe
kumquats	loquats
mandarin oranges	mangoes
nectarines	oranges
papayas	peaches
persimmons	tangerines
Spices (1 teaspoon powdered)	
mace	nutmeg
orange peel	saffron (a pinch or a few strands)

stead of pasta or bread to enhance immune response, particularly during stressful times.

Servings per Day · Choose one serving (½ cup) of orange fruit and vegetables every day. Use alkaline-buffering orange spices to flavor food and add antioxidants.

Yellow

Yellow is a predominant color found in tropical and summer fruits and vegetables. *Lutein* is a yellow carotenoid that protects

Vegetables (½ cup = 1 serving)	
corn (fresh)	crookneck squash
mushrooms	parsnips
rutabagas	shallots
yellow onions	yellow patty pan squash
yellow peppers	yellow potatoes
Fruit (½ cup = 1 serving)	
avocados	bananas
grapefruit	guavas
kadota figs	lemons
pears	pineapples
pomelos	Rainier cherries
star fruit	umeboshi plums
yellow apples	
Spices (seeds or roots) (1 teaspoon powdered)	
caraway	cardamom
coriander	cumin
curry	dill seed
fennel	fenugreek
ginger	lemon peel
mustard seed	turmeric

NOTE: *Although kale and spinach are green, they're two of the richest sources of the yellow pigments lutein and zeaxanthin.*

a small spot in the back of the eye called the *macula*. Age-related macular degeneration (AMD) is a common problem throughout the world. Lutein and its related carotenoid, *zeaxanthin*, appear to protect the eyes from AMD, a potentially blinding condition. Yellow fruits and vegetables contain several other carotenoids with broad health benefits.

Servings per Day • Choose one serving (½ cup) of yellow foods per day. Use yellow spices liberally to season food, add antioxidants, and reduce the need for salt. Yellow foods, except for the slightly acidic curry, are alkaline buffers.

Blue, Purple, and Black

The family of blue, purple, and black fruits and vegetables contains phytonutrients known as polyphenols. They pack some of the highest antioxidant power available and help rid the body of potential carcinogens. Polyphenols can also protect the vascular system, reduce allergic symptoms, curb inflammation, and inhibit tumor growth. Green and black teas also fit into this category.

Servings per Day • Your meal plans include one serving of purple fruits or vegetables. Increase the benefits of eating foods in this group by drinking tea. These foods are alkaline buffers, except for black tea and wine (organic), which are slightly acidic.

Green

The green family provides excellent phytonutrients to cleanse your body as well as most essential minerals and vitamins. Sulfur-rich vegetables, including all the cruciferous vegetables, the mustard family, and members of the garlic and onion family, help eliminate toxins and are thought to protect against several

Vegetables (½ cup = 1 serving)	
eggplant	purple cabbage
purple cauliflower	purple kale
purple Swiss chard	radicchio
purple fingerling potatoes	purple carrots
Fruit (½ cup = 1 serving)	
berry juices	bilberries
blackberries	black cherries
blueberries	boysenberries
elderberries	grape juice
green and black teas	huckleberries
lingonberries	mission figs
ollalie berries	passion fruit
purple grapes	purple plums
purple prunes	raisins
red wine	
Spices (1 teaspoon powdered)	
black mustard seed	black pepper
juniper berries	vanilla bean and extract

forms of cancer. Because of their sulfur content, these vegetables taste and look best when eaten raw or lightly steamed. High heat and prolonged cooking destroy most of their valuable enzymes and vitamins and wash out minerals in green foods, so avoid overcooking them. And vitamin C in these foods is lost during prolonged storage, so buy them as soon after they are picked as possible and use them right away.

Cruciferous vegetables (primarily broccoli, cauliflower, and members of the mustard family), radishes, jicama, and daikon make great snacks. If you don't care for raw broccoli and cauliflower, then blanch them quickly in boiling water and shock them with ice water to stop the cooking process quickly and retain most of their vitamins, minerals, and phytonutrients. With many choices among green vegetables and herbs, it's easy to include them in your daily meal plans. Choose fresh, organic greens when possible. If you are just adopting my new cuisine, try those cellophane bags of mixed baby greens to make wonderful salads. They look pretty, are good for you, and lend a creative flair to your meals. Along with a salad for dinner, it's easy to add a green vegetable and satisfy your daily green serving requirement.

SERVINGS PER DAY • Menu plans provide at least four servings (2 cups) of green fruits and vegetables. Amounts of fresh and dried herbs vary according to the recipe. Green foods are alkaline buffers. Sea vegetables are the most alkaline of all green foods.

Tan

Tan foods contain *phytosterols*, *phytoestrogens*, fiber, and *saponins* with several potential disease-preventing benefits. They are believed to help balance hormones and include vitamin E, several B vitamins, and the minerals copper, zinc, magnesium, chromium, and iron.

Grain seeds offer complete packages of vitamins and minerals to help digest stored starch and process the energy-rich sugars needed to sprout the seeds. These nutrients are stored in the outer brown layers of the grains, so refining and milling to lengthen shelf life and improve appearance removes most of those nutrients. Food fortification was instituted to offset the nutrient losses by replacing some, but not all, so the same complete package of nutrients is needed for us to digest and use the starch and sugars contained in the grain. Without them, the grains' nutritional benefits are lost and the body treats the foods differently.

Vegetables (½ cup = 1 serving)	
artichokes	arugula
asparagus	baby greens mix
braising greens (for stir frying)	broccoli
Brussels sprouts	cauliflower
collards	cucumbers
daikon	French sorrel
green beans	green cabbage
green onions (scallions)	green peas
green peppers	horseradish
kale	kohlrabi
leeks	lettuce
mustard leaves	parsley
sea vegetables	shallots
snow peas	spinach
sprouts	sugar snap peas
wasabi	watercress
zucchini	

Fruit (½ cup = 1 serving)	
avocados	green grapes
green melons	green pears (ripe)
green plums	kiwi
limes	

Fresh and Dried Herbs	
basil	bay leaves
chives	cilantro
dill weed	oregano
parsley	peppermint
rosemary	sage
savory	tarragon
thyme	wasabi
wintergreen	

Most people consume too many food items in this group, most of them in processed (white) form and containing added sugar. Cookies, chips, candy, soft drinks, ice cream, rolls, crackers, snacks, white rice, white potatoes, and pasta all contain white, refined carbohydrates. Consider where supermarkets have expanded and what is contained in those newer middle aisles. Stay clear of the middle of the store and the enticing gondolas loaded with prepared foods, and you'll avoid processed foods and sugar- and fat-laden snacks.

Another fast-growing category in supermarkets is in the quick meal category, those easy to grab and take home. But beware of these foods because most have a laundry list of chemicals you just don't need. Rely on them occasionally, provided you eat the 7-Color way most of the time and add something colorful to them for better balance. For example, pick a dinner with meat, potatoes,

Top Picks for Tan

NOTE: *Read the nutrition facts panel on the package on crackers to know the number per serving, because size varies.*

NOTE: *Any sprouted grain or legume is alkaline.*

Whole Grains (1 cup = 1 serving)	
all whole grains	brown rice
bulgur wheat	cornmeal
organic couscous	granola
kasha	oatmeal
polenta	tabouli
vegetable pasta	whole-grain flour products
whole-grain pasta	
Legumes (1 cup = 1 serving)	
beans	lentils
split peas	
Nuts, Seeds, and Nut Butters (¼ cup = 1 serving)	
flax seeds	nut butters (organic)
peanuts	sesame seeds
sunflower and poppy seeds	tahini
tree nuts (including pine nuts)	

CREATING 7-COLOR CUISINE

and gravy, but serve it with one of the wonderful, colorful salads suggested among the perfect, four-module salads in Part Two.

White, fatty, and highly processed foods have been blamed for the obesity epidemic now invading the U.S., partly because they trigger the release of two hormones that regulate sugar and fat metabolism. The first is *insulin*, which floods the system when sugary foods are eaten. One of insulin's effects is to stimulate the release of a second hormone, *cortisol*, better known as a "fight-or-flight" hormone. Among its other effects, cortisol increases fat storage and has a particular affinity for the body's mid-section. Doctors have now linked being fat around the middle to cardio-vascular disease and diabetes. In the 7-Color plan, you'll replace white foods with healthier choices in tan and brown.

Nuts and seeds have been shown to provide protection for the cardiovascular system and should be included every day. Organic nut butters are a good choice to spread on toast or use as a dip for raw vegetables, such as celery or baby carrots.

SERVINGS PER DAY • Include a combination of any two of the following whole-grain selections: 1-cup servings of grains, legumes, rice, cereals, or starchy vegetables; or two slices of bread, one whole pita, tortilla, English muffin, or bagel; or approximately six crackers. Although organic oats are not, quinoa, wild rice, grains, and legumes are slightly acidic.

Creamy White

Foods that are creamy white contain amino acids, healthy oils, and important antioxidants. Amino acids, the building blocks of protein, are important in helping replace worn-out tissues and essential in building enzymes. Scientists consider those the most important class of proteins. There are 3,870 different

Meat, Poultry, and Fish (4 ounces = 1 serving)	
all fish	all shellfish
beef	chicken
duck	eggs
game hens	lamb
lean lunch meats	pork
tofu	turkey
Dairy (1 cup = 1 serving)	
amazake	cottage cheese
kefir	milk (low-fat)
nut milk	rice milk
soft cheese	soy products
yogurt	
Oils (1 tablespoon = 1 serving) and Dressings (2 tablespoons = 1 serving)	
almond	avocado
canola	flax
hazelnut	macadamia
organic olive	organic walnut

NOTE: *Dairy products and legumes can be substituted.*

NOTE: *One teaspoon of butter can be substituted for one-half of a serving of oil or dressing.*

metabolic enzymes, each controlling a specific biochemical transformation. Some are needed to aid digestion while others shuttle nutrients to cells.

Other important members of the creamy white group of foods are healthy seed and nut oils, dairy products, soy products, cheese, and eggs. These foods help cells "talk" to one another, an essential function for them to remain healthy and disease-free. Omega-3 oils, which reduce inflammation and help block the formation of blood clots, are found in fish and also in flax, canola, macadamia, organic walnut, and organic olive oils. Limit saturated fat intake, including butter and transfat-free margarine, but do include a serving of healthy oils in cooking or on salads. Mayonnaise and salad dressings are considered oils, but they are low in saturated fats.

SERVINGS PER DAY • Include two 4-ounce servings of fish, poultry, meat, soy products, lean lunch meats, two eggs, or 4 ounces of cheese. Add two 1-cup servings of dairy products. Include 1 tablespoon of healthy oil or 2 tablespoons of dressings. You can substitute 1 teaspoon of butter or transfat-free margarine for half the oil or dressing servings, but keep this to a minimum. Meats, poultry, and fish are acidic; fish are the least acidic and red meat is the most. Oils and dairy products are neutral.

Condiments and Dipping Sauces

Avoid fat-free dressings because various forms of sugars are used to create the creamy texture that fat normally provides. Low-fat dressings are acceptable, but read labels carefully to make sure they don't contain sugar. High-fructose corn syrup, corn syrup, rice bran syrup, cane juice, fruit juice or grape concentrates, fructose, dextrose, sucrose, and maltodextrin are all forms of sugar. Low-fat dressings and lemon juice also add zest to vegetables. Look for recipes that show you how to make your own sauces, chutneys, dips, marinades, and salsas. These really can transform plain vegetables, fish, and poultry into special dishes. You'll also find a list of the best condiments and sauces under the "pantry management" section in Part 2.

Other condiments appear in many recipes and include fat-free, low-sodium soup bases, soybean miso paste, low-sodium soy (shoyu) sauce, and sea vegetables. Nori is the best-known sea vegetable because it is used to wrap sushi. Other important sea vegetables are kelp, arame, hijiki, and wakame. Add them to soups and stews for flavor. They're excellent alkalizing agents due to their high mineral content and help restore normal pH balance in those people who are acidic. Chlorella, blue-green algae, and spirulina have similar pH-balancing effects.

Herbs and Spices

Herbs and spices add protective antioxidants and zest to everything they join. Spices have been used for centuries to help preserve foods and cover the off-tastes of meat as well as to minimize indigestion caused by eating spoiled meat. While this is no longer a major problem in modern countries, using spices also reduces the craving for salt as flavoring. Marinating meat to reduce its toughness has also been a common practice over many centuries. Today the practice of marinating meats before grilling is still a great idea, but for a different reason. The spices, wines, and fruit used in marinades help reduce the harmful effects of eating blackened or charcoal-coated meat with their polyaromatic hydrocarbon (PAH) residues.

The difference between herbs and spices is somewhat arbitrary. Leaves and flowers are generally considered herbs, while seeds, bark, roots, and rhizomes are considered spices. Pungency is another factor that determines into which category a seasoning falls. For example, cloves and saffron are both flower parts, but they're considered spices. Spices commonly contain high levels of yellow, orange, and red carotenoids, while herbs contain high levels of organic acids and polyphenols. All this means is that you need both spices and herbs to enjoy their full antioxidant protection. They are also alkaline, so use them generously.

Using herbs and spices with a particular theme is fun and adds interest to meals. My favorites include barbecue seasoning, bouquet garni, Cajun seasoning, Chesapeake Bay seasoning, chili powder blends, Chinese five spice, curry powder blends, fines herbes, Greek seasoning, Italian seasoning, jerk seasoning, Mexican seasoning, mulling spices, and poultry seasoning.

Servings per day include ¼ to 1 teaspoon, depending on the recipe. Use pepper in most meals, because it helps digestion. Please don't add salt at the table, and use it sparingly in recipes. The recipes here require less than half the amount of salt normally found in recipes because we use herbs and spices generously to add that flavorful zing. The recipes also call for RealSalt, which contains trace amounts of minerals in addition to sodium, or 4/S salt, which is a little lower in sodium (390 milligrams versus 530 per ¼ teaspoon) because other spices have been blended in. Another favorite blend for seasoning is gomasio, a Japanese blend of sesame seeds, seaweed, and sea salt. It contains a mere 35 milligrams of sodium per ½ teaspoon.

Now let's get started.

A New Way of Eating

CHAPTER FOUR

Step One: Get Set

E MBRACING THE 7-COLOR CUISINE plan is fun, but I realize that dietary change, no matter how simple, requires motivation and commitment.

My clients' satisfaction with the plan increases in direct proportion to their motivations for undertaking it. They're asked to make a three-month commitment, the time needed to achieve significant results, but most people have been amazed to experience benefits in just two or three weeks. Most have been so happy with the results, they've continued to practice 7-Color Cuisine. An occasional slip and return to old habits doesn't set them back unless they persist with those habits for a month or more. But even then, their return to the plan quickly corrects the inevitable, unwelcome symptoms encountered when they strayed from it.

Finding Your Motivation

What's your motivation for seeking change? Are you willing to give this plan a try for three months? Look over the following list of the most common complaints my clients reported before they began to eat my way:

+ Doctor advised dietary change
+ Gas
+ Digestive problems
+ Inflammation
+ Aching joints
+ Cramps
+ Constipation

- Frequent diarrhea
- Obesity
- Water retention
- Low energy
- Chronic sinus condition
- Excessive mucus
- Allergies
- Forgetfulness
- High cholesterol
- High blood pressure
- Anxiety
- Jumpiness, nervousness
- Mood swings
- Insomnia
- Easily distracted

Write down the complaints that apply to you and also record any other condition you have that's not listed. Your list will become the benchmark for measuring your personal success with the 7-Color plan.

It's important, too, to identify your specific motivation for undertaking this, or any, change. Add your written reasons to your list.

If being overweight is one of the problems you've listed, then you'll lose weight even though this is not a weight-loss scheme or fad diet. Eating 7-Color Cuisine will result in a gradual but steady loss of extra pounds. As potential proof, try on a too-snug pair of pants now and try them on again at the end of your first month on the plan. And put away the scale, because it doesn't tell the whole story and can give a false impression of how you're doing.

Some of my clients work with personal trainers as they embrace the plan, and they sometimes gain weight. That's because they're increasing lean muscle mass while burning fat. These folks slim down in all the right places and attain firmer contours. To be successful with any weight loss program, you need to walk or add other aerobic exercise.

The New Barbara in Just Twenty-one Days

Barbara, who has type-II diabetes, was advised by her doctor to try my dietary regimen and her results were startling. In just twenty-one days, she dropped two pant sizes and reported significantly greater energy. She felt much more motivated to eat right and believed that her mood swings ceased. Chronic sinus problems that had plagued Barbara for years were alleviated, and her blood sugar dropped from 200 (in mg/dl) to normal (the normal, fasting blood glucose level is 70–100 mg/dl). Barbara's doctor reported that he was able to reduce her medication and finally control her diabetes with my dietary regimen alone.

An Athlete with Bad Digestion

Digestive problems are a common complaint, and Steve is a prime example of how the 7-Color plan can help correct indigestion. Steve never went anywhere without antacids. A sports enthusiast, he wanted to improve his diet to meet his training goals. He also wanted to reduce that frequent indigestion because he realized it was interfering with the absorption and utilization of nutrients. He enthusiastically embraced the 7-Color plan and made sure to eat 7 colors a day and get the freshest organic produce from a local farm market. He ate more slowly and was mindful of the importance in chewing every bite carefully and thoughtfully. Steve's wife enjoyed making new meals according to the plan with him, a practice they've continued to now include their toddler son.

The plan's simple steps have led Steve to total freedom from antacids. He has more energy, stamina, and increased focus to help him also meet his training goals.

Attitudes about Eating

Many people I work with don't even want to think about food, which they view as the enemy. Taste buds conditioned to salty and sweet flavors lose their ability to pick up the subtleties of fresh fruit and vegetables. But it takes just a few days of eating 7-Color Cuisine for your sensitivity to fresh tastes to return.

Fad Diets Just Did Not Work for Jenny

Jenny was a yo-yo dieter for many years and tried all the fad diets. Each led to initial weight loss, but then she'd hit a plateau, become discouraged, and quit. She tried stimulants, but they made her jumpy. The extra weight always returned, and she came to view mealtime as something to be dreaded. Within the first week of embracing the 7-Color plan, Jenny was surprised at how much more energy and mental clarity she had. For the first time in several months she slept through the night. Jenny began to enjoy her meals and savor the beauty of the fresh, colorful meals she made and presented for her family and friends. Best of all, she experienced a steady weight loss, and the pounds stayed off. Today she loves the way she feels and looks.

A Smoker's Dream Nutrition Plan

Just as overweight people lose taste sensation, so do smokers. My case studies show that those who quit smoking and embrace 7-Color Cuisine are less likely to experience weight gain, a common occurrence in those who substitute salty and/or sweet snacks for cigarettes when they quit. When you smoke, the body's acidity increases. The foods in this plan supply buffering agents that counter that acidity and help reduce nicotine cravings as your body regains better balance.

Natalie smoked, she thought, to help her concentrate when working at her computer, yet she had low energy, trouble sleeping, and was easily distracted. Although she wasn't overweight, her body was out of condition and not as shapely as she wanted it to be. She was also plagued with digestive problems, common symptoms of an overly acidic condition.

Within the first month of beginning the 7-Color plan, Natalie was sleeping well enough to require fewer hours of sleep. Her digestion improved and she began to lose tummy and thigh fat. Her concentration improved dramatically, as did her energy level. She reduced her cigarette-dependency and was able to quit entirely within a few months. Then a major upheaval in her personal life and a new high-stress job sent Natalie back to smoking and grabbing whatever was handy to eat. But this time, when those annoying symptoms surfaced, she quickly returned to the 7-Color plan and again enjoyed its benefits to her whole body, mind, and spirit. She stuck with the program and remains a nonsmoker.

What Do You Need to Change?

What's your attitude about meal planning? Appendix A contains a meal diary to help you identify habits you want to change and that need changing. Use this diary for a week, and you'll find that you have fully evaluated those habits. But right now, take a minute to honestly answer the following questions.

1. Do you:
    a. Generally eat all that is on your plate?
    b. Eat small servings?
    c. Eat second servings frequently?
    d. Eat a wide variety of foods?

      e. Feel satisfied when you finish a meal?

      f. Find meals you fix at home boring?

      g. Ask for a "doggie bag" when dining out? (Some people are embarrassed to do this; don't be one of them.)

      h. Have regular mealtimes?

      i. Eat only when really hungry?

      j. Eat breakfast?

      k. Love snacks?

      l. Eat on the run (for example, while driving)?

      m. Stand when eating?

      n. Eat alone often?

2. How long does it take you to finish your meals?

3. Does your family eat together? If not, take a minute to state why not.

4. What's your favorite snack? How often do you eat it?

5. Is there a food that you must eat every day in order to feel good? What is it?

Questions 1a through 1g relate to portion control and your use of take-home containers. Most people put too much food on a plate, as you know from Part One where I explain how using a smaller plate and covering only the center of the plate with the main course works better. *Side* dishes such as vegetables and salads are just that. They go beside the main course plate.

When you eat out, eat as well as you can, according to the 7-Color plan. Enjoy your choice, but also evaluate the quality of ingredients in your meal when it's served and decide at the start that you might want to eat some and take the rest home. If the serving is large, and more than you know you should eat, then pick out the colorful parts of the meal and leave less nutritious ingredients behind.

Many restaurants serve large plates with less expensive ingredients such as pasta or lettuce topped with small amounts of the ingredients that are more colorful and appealing. Plates heaping with food look like a lot for your money, but if you really look at what you're being served, you can easily reinforce selective eating and curtail your own overconsumption of less nutritious foods. Large portions may seem like a good value at the time, but you will wind up wearing the extra value around your middle.

Questions 1h through 1j relate to good digestion. Regular mealtimes that include well-thought-out menu plans encourage a healthy appetite for good food.

Our bodies operate with a set of biorhythms that anticipate food at regular intervals. Maximum digestive benefits are achieved when we honor them. People who don't have regular mealtimes are more likely to grab whatever's handy or eat when they're not really hungry.

Breakfast is known to be one of the most important meals of the day. How your break the overnight fast in the morning can make a big difference in how you experience the day ahead of you.

Heading out the door with a cup of coffee and a white-flour, sugar-filled something won't help support good cognitive function and has been proved to set you up for later energy and stress-level plunges. You really must include good quality protein at breakfast to function optimally, and it's not difficult to eat a more healthy and satisfying breakfast.

Questions 1k through 1n identify the need for you to eat with the 7-Color plan on a regular basis for better health.

Of course you're going to take an occasional trip to the drive-up window, and that's fine, provided you stick to the 7-Color plan and work with it most of the time, but too many of us depend on fast foods daily without fully realizing how often we do so. We pull up and even buy meals now on credit for our toddlers, and we do them such a disservice when we feed them that way. The commercial appeal of advertising and getting little gifts from national chain drive-ins is fun, but we owe it to our children to control how and what they eat.

And that includes caring enough to make home-cooked meals more fun and appealing according to the plan, which makes it easy. Reinforce to your children the science of eating more healthy snacks and drinking lots of pure water and you'll find they, too, become reconditioned to want to eat better. Having good stuff on hand for your kids to snack on means you're all on the right track.

Questions 2 and 3 relate to Step Four, which celebrates the enjoyment of meals with people you love.

In the past, dinner became the most important meal for American families because this was the time when most family members gathered. Now, many after-school sports and other activities overlap the traditional dinner hour.

Researchers at Rutgers University analyzed the eating habits among more than 18,000 adolescents and found that those who ate dinner with their parents consumed more fruits, vegetables, and dairy foods than those who did not.

The last three questions concern your favorite "comfort foods." You surely have certain foods or beverages that you feel almost addicted to, and it will take time and patience to give them up. These questions help you identify what they are. Then you'll work to *slowly* eliminate them from your diet. If you eliminate them too quickly, you'll feel deprived; and that's not what the 7-Color plan wants.

Once you've identified all your attitudes about food, you can formulate a plan to change them. This is the time to remove snacks and less nutritious items from your refrigerator, freezer, and pantry and replace them with healthier choices.

Appendix B contains a model nutrition fact panel with notes highlighting what to look for on labels when you shop. There are four main, unhealthy ingredients that you must scan labels for: salt, saturated fats, transfats, and sugars and synthetic sweeteners.

Transfats are a particularly nasty saturated fat found in foods made with hydrogenated or partially hydrogenated oils. Hydrogenation turns oil into fat that remains solid at room temperature and gives foods a creamy, pleasing texture and longer shelf life. Most snack foods, cookies, crackers, and many spreads, such as peanut butter and margarine, contain transfats. Experts consider transfats deleterious to cardiovascular health, and believe they may contribute to certain types of cancer. Labeling transfats will become mandatory in January 2006, but until then, look for un-saturated and monounsaturated fats on labels to know that those foods contain few, if any, transfats and are good choices.

Confused about "Freshness"?

The widespread use of preservatives to extend shelf life in pack-aged baked goods has confused us about what constitutes fresh-ness. I'll never forget a conversation that explains what I mean. The woman sitting next to me at a recent luncheon asked another woman about her new job at a well-known national cookie com-pany. The cookie-company woman answered with enthusiasm about the purchase of a new line of bakery products that boasted an eighteen-week shelf life. In her view, that made those pastries "the very freshest," but to me it was amazing to think that anyone could think of a food sitting on the shelf unchanged for eighteen weeks as fresh.

Making Your Shopping Lists

Now that you've decided what will be the best time to go shopping, you can make appropriate lists for what you need. Make copies of your lists and keep them handy to replace individual items as you use them to save considerable time and stress by keeping staples and bottled items on hand. You'll find several specific shopping lists in Appendix C, but start thinking to organize your staples into your cold pantry for refrigerated items, your dry pantry for staples, your wet pantry for canned or bottled items, and your stocks of beverages, spices, herbs, and other seasonings. You can conveniently and inexpensively get the spices from Penzey's Spices, for one source, on the Internet without ever leaving your home.

Use Step Three to check the fresh ingredients you need for the weekly recipes on your cold-pantry shopping list. Choose to divide your shopping for fresh items into two weekly trips, or visit the markets weekly and freeze fish, poultry, or meats you'll need later that week.

Part of what makes using the 7-Color plan easy is that you don't have to hunt for anything if you keep your pantries—and they can be large or small—well-stocked with the listed items to prepare various healthy, fun meals.

CHAPTER FIVE

Step Two: Go Shopping

Pantry Makeover

Removing unwanted items from your shelves, refrigerator, and freezer will take a little time, but it's the only way to make sure you have only those things on hand that are good for you and that you need for recipes. Go into this with the idea that you're making a fresh start, just as you would when moving from one home to the next. We begin by clearing the refrigerator and freezer: your cold pantry.

Cold Pantry

You'll need to buy five of the 7-Color foods fresh two times each week. Carrots, onions, potatoes, citrus fruits, and apples are exceptions that you can keep for longer periods of time, but these should still be eaten as close to their purchase as possible. Items you'll need for the week are listed with that week's menu plans.

Begin by cleaning the refrigerator and throwing out any produce you have stored. Next, go through bottled items and toss any with just small amounts remaining or that you've had for more than one month. Read the labels on the bottled items you want to save, but make extra-sure to check those labels with the nutrition facts panel information in Appendix B.

Foods to be stored in the cold pantry include dairy products, produce, fresh fruits and vegetables, fresh fruit juice, and freezer items.

Make copies of the cold-pantry shopping list in Appendix C and keep it in mind when you shop for cold-pantry foods.

DAIRY PRODUCTS ◆ A wide choice of dairy products, including goat's milk, soy milk, rice milk and nut milks, is available when you shop. Your choices for soy, rice, and nut milks should be fortified with calcium and vitamin A to bring them closer to the nutrition content of cow or goat's milk. You'll also want to check the protein content on rice and nut beverage labels, because these drinks are higher in natural sugars and lower in protein than dairy products. They can still be used in recipes calling for milk and will add interesting flavor.

Select cheeses for snacking that have less than 8 grams of fat. Hard cheeses with more than 8 grams of fat, such as Parmesan, can be used for grating because smaller quantities are used in recipes. Avoid processed cheeses entirely.

Choose plain or unsweetened yogurt, and buy those that contain live cultures. Add your own fresh fruit. Use yogurt as a topping instead of sour cream. You'll find yogurt used in breakfast smoothie recipes. Yogurt, an excellent food with a long history of use in many cultures and in folk medicine, has been credited with conferring longevity. And it's easier to digest than cow's milk and is well tolerated by most people who cannot drink milk.

PRODUCE ◆ Produce is the most interesting section of the store. You will want to concentrate your shopping there. The produce shopping list in Appendix C contains fruits and vegetables listed by color. Not all of the selections will be available year-round, particularly in farmers' markets. For example, during winter months you'll find an abundance of cruciferous vegetables, carrots and other root vegetables, garlic, onions, leeks, dark leafy greens such as spinach, kale, Swiss chard, anise (fennel) bulb, collards, mustard greens, and bok choy. You'll also find lots of winter squash, sweet potatoes, yams, red potatoes, Asian eggplant, cilantro, French sorrel, winter apples, pears, dates, and nuts. Avocados and citrus fruit are plentiful during winter months; as spring looms, you'll find strawberries, artichokes, asparagus, kiwi, and figs.

Summer markets offer many kinds of squash, tomatoes, basil, spicy and sweet peppers, eggplant, leafy green lettuce in many colors, scallions, shallots, corn, peas, green beans, melons, berries, apricots, peaches, cherries, and grapes. The selections will vary by where you live, so this is meant to be a shopping guideline. Change your vegetable and fruit choices seasonally for the best nutritional and taste advantage.

Take the time to wash and get your vegetables ready for storage when you get home. Wash leafy greens and spinach by submerging them in cold water in the sink. You can also add a few drops of biodegradable vegetable wash to remove residues. Gently swish the leaves after separating them from the core or stem. Lift them out of the water and check to make sure they're clean. If the green leaves are small, as are baby spinach and mesclun leaves, use a salad spinner to dry them, then store them in a covered container in the refrigerator. If you have just one-half pound of small greens, they'll fit in the salad spinner and can be cleaned easily before storage. Larger leaves can be arranged around the perimeter of the spinner and spun to remove most of the water. Lay the spun leaves out on a layer of paper towels to dry for a short time. Then roll up the towel around the leaves and place it in a plastic bag in the refrigerator. Cut the tops from root vegetables; using a vegetable brush, lightly brush them under running water. Keep the skin intact, because it contains antioxidants that prevent spoiling. Removing surface dirt cuts the number of soil bacteria and other microorganisms that would otherwise hasten spoiling.

Most fruits and fresh local tomatoes should not be refrigerated. Buy just enough to last until you shop again. Berries do need refrigeration. Wash them first, let them dry a bit, and store them in a paper towel–lined bowl with a loose plastic cover. These simple procedures keep your greens fresh and crisp and your fruits and vegetables ready to prepare; the steps will save valuable time when preparing meals.

Freezer

Most home freezers are self-defrosting and don't store frozen foods well for extended periods. Repeated defrosting and refreezing food causes "freezer burn," which spoils the food. Plan on eating items that defrost easily, such as green peas, green beans, and corn kernels, within one month. If you open a package of vegetables and they're whitish, discard them. Vegetables that have been stored too long in the freezer also have an unpleasant odor. Larger foods such as fish, poultry, and meats are less likely to defrost and may be stored for as long as three months and longer if kept in a non–self-defrosting freezer. Whole grains and whole-grain flours can be stored in tightly closed containers in the freezer to slow rancidity, but they're also subject to freezer burn and should not be stored more than three months.

If it's convenient for you to keep large quantities of frozen food on hand, then consider investing in a freezer that's not self-defrosting. You'll be able to keep items frozen solid for longer periods of time.

Dry Pantry

Maintaining your well-stocked dry pantry is the key to easy meal preparation. Here are the food items that you store on shelves in a cool, dry place in or near your kitchen. Many will be stored in their original containers, others will require repackaging in containers with tight lids. As you remove products containing preservatives and hydrogenated fats from shelves and replace them with more natural items, you'll need to be more vigilant about making sure they're stored properly. Whole grains and their products become stale and rancid over time. Moths and bugs love natural foods, so you'll have to protect them against infestation. Here are tips for storing your dry pantry items.

WHOLE GRAINS ✦ Whole grains include brown rice, wild rice, barley, bulgur wheat, buckwheat groats (kasha), polenta (coarse cornmeal), millet, and organic couscous, a semolina product. Try to purchase whole grains that are organic. Whole grains are used as accompaniments to main courses, can be added to soups, and make wonderful, nutritious leftovers for breakfast or lunch. They're easily enhanced with chicken or beef broth, mushrooms, vegetables, onions, nuts, seeds, and herbs. Cooking time for whole grains is longer than for white rice—approximately 45 minutes—so they should be placed in a steamer soon after you get home from work or prepared the night before and reheated at mealtime. Once rice is steaming, don't stir it in the pot until all moisture is absorbed, because it will become sticky.

Many health-conscious people cook more rice than is needed for one meal and store extra servings in the refrigerator for quick and easy meal preparation later. Along with beans, whole grains supply the major source of protein in the purest of vegetarian diets, that is, vegan diets. You can also cook whole grains on top of the stove or in a pressure cooker. Grains that are cut, such as kasha, organic couscous, steel-cut organic oats, and polenta will clog the steam vent in a pressure cooker and should not be cooked this way.

Whole grains should be removed from their packages once they are opened. Place them in glass or plastic jars with snugly fitting lids. Plan to use them within one year (or sooner in hot climates). In dry, hot climates, grains lose moisture, even when stored in their original packages or containers with tight lids, and will take longer to cook. Along with loss of moisture go flavor and nutrition.

Look for expiration dates on packages of whole grains, just as you would dairy products, and don't buy them if they're outdated. You'll find that some stores are better about watching pull dates on products than others are. Support the local natural food retailer who's most conscientious about maintaining freshness.

If you've had a container of grains around for a while and aren't sure about freshness, check the odor when you remove the cap. Fresh grains have a pleasant, earthy, and sometimes aromatic odor. Rancid grains have a pungent smell and shouldn't be used. Use this same technique when buying whole grains that you package yourself from bulk bins. It's also a good idea to make up your own freshness dating system by writing the date you open the package on its storage container.

Legumes • Legumes, peas, and beans are some of the most versatile foods you can add to your diet. They're extremely good sources of proteins and serve as nutritional complements to rice. They also contain valuable phytonutrients that protect you. Soybeans and products made from them are extremely popular as hormone-balancing foods.

Beans come in all colors, sizes, and shapes. It's fun to have an assortment on display in tall jars just for visual effect. Legumes can be difficult to digest, especially if you don't eat them frequently. Split peas, lentils, and lima beans are less apt to cause gas and bloating, so it's best to start with them. Beans need to be well cooked, and soaking them before cooking helps reduce gas. I also add herbs, either *epazote* (a Mexican herb) or *ajwain* (from Pakistan), to cooking water to help break down the complex sugars in beans that we can't digest. Soybeans contain *protease inhibitors*, types of protein that prevent enzymes from breaking down the bean before it sprouts. Cooking disables these proteins, which is why soybeans are cooked. An excellent way to cook all beans is in a pressure cooker. Most beans require soaking, but then take just 10 to 15 minutes to cook. Split peas, lentils, and black-eyed peas don't require soaking. Heirloom varieties such as Yellow Indian Woman beans, cranberry beans, and black lentils are making their way back to farmers' markets. They may require less cooking time.

Beans can be added to salad for extra protein or prepared as delicious spreads such as hummus (chickpea spread). Miso is a fermented paste made from soybeans that makes terrific marinades and dressings. It's also an ideal vegetarian seasoning in soups and casseroles. Miso soup is generally served at the beginning of a Japanese meal and is an excellent snack or pick-me-up during the day.

CEREALS ✦ Cereals have the same storage requirements as whole grains do. Generally, a box of cereal is eaten quickly and long before it becomes rancid. You can fold down the inner bag, put a clip on it, and push it down in the box, but granola, cracked wheat, multigrain cereals, and rolled oats will need to be stored in glass containers with tight lids. If you plan to keep them a while, you can also store them in the freezer in snug containers.

FLOUR   •   Whole-grain flour can turn rancid quickly, and you may find it best to store in the freezer for up to one year. If you suspect it's old, then do the sniff test on the container when you open it. Fresh flour has a pleasant nutty odor, while rancid flour smells pungent. Once a bag of whole-grain flour is opened, it's best to transfer the contents into a plastic or glass container with a tight lid.

SUGAR AND SWEETENERS   •   There are many kinds of sweeteners, both natural and synthetic. The latest synthetic sweetener to appear on the market is sucralose, marketed as Splenda. It's advertised with the slogan, "Made from sugar so it tastes like sugar," but, unlike table sugar, which metabolizes into calories and carbohydrates, Splenda is not digested. It doesn't appear to alter blood glucose levels, at least short-term, which makes it attractive to diabetics.

Nevertheless, many nutritionists question Splenda's long-term health effects and worry that Americans will think they have a green light to eat as many sweetened foods as they like. Because the average American eats 158 pounds of sugar per year, substituting Splenda could result in substantial intake of the artificial sweetener. Colas are one of the items most commonly sweetened with Splenda and are advertised as low-carb and low-calorie, which makes them seem more appealing. But the problem of mineral depletion by these beverages is being completely overlooked, and merely changing the sweetener does nothing to reduce bone thinning.

Splenda's biggest drawback is an aftertaste, and it does not have the same browning and baking properties as sugar. To counter this, McNeil Nutritionals, its manufacturer, offers a 50:50 baking blend of sugar and Splenda containing half the calories of pure sugar.

Polyols are a group of alcohol sugars, derived from dietary sugar, which are not completely absorbed. They're found in many of the foods we eat and are also created naturally in the human body. Polyols include mannitol, maltitol, sorbitol, zylitol, and erythritol. Only two of the polyols, mannitol and erythritol, have zero caloric value. The others, except for maltitol, have lower caloric and glycemic index values than sugar. Sugar alcohols such as sorbitol and xylitol have been used for many years to sweeten dietetic foods and don't affect blood sugar levels. Xylitol is known for its anticavity effects, while the other polyols have no effect on dental health. Polyols haven't been used long enough to determine their long-term safety, but some have been approved for use in dietetic foods with few, if any, reported side effects. Table 5-1 shows the glycemic index value and calories of each of the polyols. The last entry is table sugar for comparison.

Natural sugars and sweeteners come in many forms. Table 5-2 lists them with concise information about each. Although many

TABLE 5-1 *Glycemic Index Values and Calories of Polyols*

NOTE: *Glycemic index is a measure of the ability of a food to raise blood sugar levels as compared to glucose. Table adapted from Geoffrey Livesey,* Nutrition Research Reviews, *2003; 16:163–191.*

Polyol	Glycemic Index (%)	Calories per Gram
Erythritol	0	1.5
Isomalt	9	2.5
Lactitol	6	2
Maltitol	36	2.7
Maltitol syrup	36–53 (high)	2.7–3
Mannitol	0	1.5
Polyglycitol (hydrogenated starch hydrolysate)	39	2.8
Sorbitol	9	2.5
Xylitol	13	3
Sugar (glucose)	100	4

TABLE 5-2 *Natural Sugars and Sweeteners*

Sugar or Sweetener	Origin and Use	Sugars (g/tsp.)
Barley malt	Natural sugar from sprouted barley. Can be used at table, in beverages, or substituted for half the sugar in any recipe.	< 1
Beet sugar	Sugar derived from sugar beets instead of sugar cane. A useful alternative for those with allergies to cane sugar. Can be used as a substitute for sugar in any application.	4
Date sugar	Natural sugar from dates. Can be used at table, in beverages, as a topping, or as a substitute for sugar in any recipe.	2
Dextrose	Simple sugar equivalent to glucose. Gives an instant burst of energy, generally reserved for sports applications. Equivalent to glucose on the glycemic index. Derived from corn.	3
Erythritol	Noncaloric polyol sweetener; can be used at table or in recipes. Occurs naturally in fruits; derived from corn.	0
Fructose	Simple sugar commonly found in fruit and derived from corn. Metabolizes more slowly than table sugar. Nearly twice as sweet as sugar, so use only half as much at table or in recipes.	4
Lactose	Natural sugar from whey; encourages growth of beneficial bacteria. Generally added to beverages for children. May be irritating to adults with lactose intolerance. Approximately 20% as sweet as sugar.	4
Sorbitol	Natural polyol sweetener found in fruits and berries. Metabolized slowly and suitable for most people with sugar problems. Derived from glucose; 75% as sweet as table sugar. Can be used at table or in any recipe that calls for sugar.	4
Stevia	Not classified as a sweetener, but a substitute for sweetening beverages; 150 to 400 times sweeter than sugar, so little is required. No long-term studies have been done on safety.	0
Sucanat	Whole natural cane sugar with water removed; used as replacement for white or brown sugar in any recipe. Alkaline forming (sugar is acidic), so excellent substitute for sugar. Retains vitamins and minerals naturally found in sugar cane.	3
Turbinado	Partially refined sugar in which two-thirds of original molasses has been removed. More flavorful than sugar and can be used at table or in any recipe that calls for sugar.	4
Xylitol	Natural polyol found in fruit; derived from corn. Has one-third fewer calories than sugar and does not raise blood sugar levels. Great sugar substitute for any sugar-free recipe. May inhibit cavities because it does not supply bacteria with fuel needed to erode tooth enamel.	2.4

come from natural sources and may retain nutrients and natural flavors not found in regular sugar, most are still forms of sugar and should be used sparingly.

An interesting herb that happens to have a sweet taste is stevia, an extract prepared from a South American herb, *Stevia rebaudiana*. It doesn't affect blood glucose, has no caloric value, and may be an alternative for sweetening beverages. However, stevia has

A NEW WAY OF EATING

not been approved by the U.S. Food and Drug Administration as a sweetener and doesn't have a sufficient history as a sweetener to justify its widespread use. Occasional use may not be harmful.

PASTA ♦ Pasta is one of the world's most beloved food products. It's incredibly easy to create wonderful meals using pasta as a base, but you'll need to develop a sense of proportion when fixing pasta dishes. When pasta dishes are served, there should be approximately equal proportions of pasta to other ingredients such as vegetables, fish, meat, and sauce.

A Doctor's Conundrum

Stewart is a physician who found it particularly difficult to prepare healthful meals because he lives alone. He maintains an extremely busy practice and has irregular working hours when he's on call. He had discovered that he didn't digest meat well and was trying a vegetarian diet. But with an overemphasis on pasta, he was getting too few vegetables to balance his high-carbohydrate diet. He was also getting too little protein and was avoiding oils in an effort to keep his weight under control. As a result he was tired, nervous, and unfocused and continued to gain weight. He was amazed when he switched to whole-grain pasta, which is more filling than white pasta, and kept appropriate proportions to vegetables. He lost weight, had more energy, and was more highly motivated. He also made sure to eat at least 12 ounces of fish each week. Fish oils supply the fatty acids needed for optimum brain function. What really impressed Stewart was that he no longer needed to rely on coffee and other caffeine-containing beverages and stimulants to keep him going.

Vegetables, herbs, organic olive oil, and pasta are natural partners that are very easy to prepare into tasty meals. The

Linguini with Vegetable Sauté

SERVINGS
2

NUTRITION FACTS

calories	656
total fat	10.9 grams
saturated fat	2.2 grams
cholesterol	5 milligrams
sodium	1201 milligrams
carbohydrate	114.3 grams
fiber	15.5 grams
protein	25.5 grams

INGREDIENTS

½ **pound organic baby spinach**

½ **pound assorted summer squash (zucchini, yellow crookneck, patty pan)**

¼ **pound portobello mushrooms, sliced**

4 **cloves garlic, put through a garlic press (try big chunks of elephant garlic)**

6 **shallots, peeled and sliced**

1½ **cups assorted bell peppers (yellow, red, orange, green), chopped**

1 **cup fresh basil leaves, chopped**

3 **sprigs fresh oregano, leaves stripped from stems**

1 **large tomato, chopped**

1 **tablespoon organic extra virgin olive oil**

1 **teaspoon black pepper, freshly ground**

½ **cup dry white wine**

½ **pound whole-grain linguini**

1 **teaspoon salt**

2 **tablespoons parmesan cheese, grated**

DIRECTIONS

1. In a large wok, lightly sauté all vegetables and herbs, tossing frequently until mixed, coated with oil, and almost cooked. Spinach and herbs should be softer.

2. Add wine and heat until it bubbles; turn down the heat, and let vegetables and wine simmer until vegetables are tender, but still crisp.

3. Meanwhile, bring a pot of salted water to boil, add linguini, and cook according to package directions.

4. When linguini is done al dente, drain and add it to the vegetable sauté without rinsing. The linguini will soak up the juices, making it more flavorful.

5. Top each of two portions with half of the grated cheese and serve.

vegetables and herbs make their own "sauce" that turns pasta like linguini into elegant dishes. Stewart found the following recipe to be simple and quick to fix, yet appealing with its many colors and added nutrition.

There is an endless variety of ways to prepare this meal. You can vary the vegetables in winter, using a combination of braising greens (kale, baby beet tops, mustard leaves, baby chard), arugula, French sorrel, butternut squash, chili peppers, fresh ginger root, and leeks. I like to top this with crumbled feta cheese. You can also add clams, salmon, tuna, white fish, or chicken to any vegetable and pasta combination.

Initially you may find that whole-grain pasta is difficult to adjust to because most of us are used to pasta made with white flour. Take it slowly and try some of the delicious vegetable pastas made from spinach, tomatoes, and beets. Smoked salmon farfalle is also delicious. The more colorful pasta in unusual forms such as rotini, radiatore, alphabets, shells, and golden quinoa elbows used in salads and soups or as side dishes may be the best way to become accustomed to the more robust flavor of whole-grain pastas.

But once you acquire a taste for the nutty, satisfying flavor of vegetable and whole-grain pasta, you won't like the white stuff. On a special note, eating more high-quality durum semolina pasta is a step in the right direction. Look for brands made from organic durum wheat. Keep portions under control and make sure the ratio is one part pasta to one part vegetables. Also consider using organic couscous, made from semolina flour.

NUTS AND SEEDS • Whole and raw nuts and seeds keep longer than roasted and salted varieties. New crops of organic walnuts found in farmers' markets in the fall need to be refrigerated or they'll get moldy. Store nuts and seeds in containers just large enough to hold them and make sure the caps are tight. Plan on using them within three months unless they're refrigerated. Just as with whole grains, nuts and seeds will turn rancid and acquire pungent odors. Don't eat them if this happens.

A large and continuing study of male health professionals in Boston, Massachusetts, has found that men who eat several servings of nuts each week are less likely to have heart attacks. This research suggests that organic walnuts, which contain high levels of cardio-friendly omega-3 fatty acids, are the most protective. Macadamia nuts and oil contain even higher levels of omega-3 acids. This healthy oil is gaining popularity, not only because of its health benefits, but also because of its wonderful buttery flavor. Be sure to buy unfiltered, unprocessed macadamia nut oil.

Nuts and seeds make great snacks and salad toppings, as you'll find out in Part Three.

DRIED VEGETABLES AND FRUIT • Marinated, dried tomatoes are a wonderful addition to pasta dishes, casseroles, and salads. They're higher in lycopene, the beneficial red pigment, than fresh tomatoes are. Because they've been harvested at the peak of the season, their flavor is superb and their nutrient levels are highest. Several other dried vegetables are readily available, including taro root, green peas, green beans, corn, and sweet and chili peppers. Mixes of these dried vegetables make good snacks and can be used to top salads as well. Look for brands without added salt or reduced salt content.

Dried fruit has been a dietary mainstay for years. Raisins, prunes, figs, and dates are the most common, but apricots, apples, pineapple, peaches, cranberries, and cherries are also popular.

Candied ginger adds excitement to salads, but use it sparingly, because it's sugarcoated.

Cranberries and cherries add that just-right touch of color to make salads more appealing and help complete your color palette for the day. Most dried fruit doesn't contain added sugar, but some does, so watch out for this. Sour fruits, such as cranberries, will usually be sweetened, but sugar shouldn't be included as one of the main ingredients.

You eat less of a dried fruit than a fresh one because removing water makes it more concentrated. Dried fruits are high in fiber and retain most of nutrients found in fresh fruits. Dried fruit, however, accounts for less than 1 percent of the total fruit consumed in the American diet, according to scientists at the University of Scranton, Pennsylvania. Their 2005 study suggests that increased consumption of dried fruit can significantly increase the body's total antioxidant capacity. Fruits that are dried without sulfur will naturally darken. Those that retain their fresh colors have most likely been treated with sulfur dioxide and should be avoided.

Wet or Liquid Pantry

Bottled and canned goods make up the wet or liquid pantry and help make foods tastier and more nutritious. They're needed staples for the recipes in this and other cookbooks and include such things as sauces, condiments, mustard, oils, vinegar, nut butters, and various beverages. Aseptic packs of soups, juices, soy milk, rice milk, and nut milks are also found in the wet pantry.

CONDIMENTS AND SAUCES ✦ In choosing bottled condiments and sauces, scrutinize labels for added sugars such as corn syrup, which is commonly included. Pick those that don't contain sweeteners; these include salsas, vegetable relishes, mustards, sugar-free ketchup and barbecue sauces, and pasta sauces. A favorite seasoning is low-salt Shoji or soy sauce.

You'll find recipes for several tasty dipping sauces in Part Three that don't contain sugar; you can substitute any of the low-calorie natural sweeteners listed above. Salad dressings fit into this category as well, although most will need refrigeration once opened.

CANNED OR BOTTLED ITEMS ◆ Most canned foods are loaded with salt and several forms of sugar such as corn syrup, evaporated cane juice, molasses, and honey. Salt-free items are appearing on grocery shelves with increasing frequency, and the low-carb trend of recent years has produced a growing number of artificially sweetened food. Most home pantries are packed with canned items, soups, vegetables, fruit, beans, sauces, condiments, beverages, sodas, oils, dressings, jams, toppings, and syrup. Stocking some of these items saves trips to the store, but you must be discriminating about which items to stock in your pantry.

FISH ◆ Canned fish, including anchovies, sardines, tuna, salmon, and oysters, often contain some sweetener and salt, but the omega-3 fatty acids they contain are so valuable that you should always have them on hand. Allow 250 milligrams of salt per serving, which equals 10 percent of your suggested daily intake. If you're not consuming other salty foods, then this need not be a huge concern. Because fish is high in protein, the glycemic effect of the sugar it contains is offset. Look for canned fish containing the least amount of sugar.

VEGETABLES AND LEGUMES   ◆   The emphasis in 7-Color Cuisine is on fresh vegetables, but a few canned vegetables should be included in your pantry for last-minute additions to meals or to boost protein intake. Limit canned vegetables to tomatoes and tomato products, beets, string beans, artichoke hearts, mushrooms, pumpkin, yams, and corn. Several are good toppings for salads, and others can be added to main dishes. Canned vegetable juices are good; just make sure to select low-salt varieties.

Several kinds of legumes, including garbanzo beans, kidney beans, and black beans, make good additions to salads. Pinto beans, lentils, and cannellini beans can be added to soup. Fat-free refried beans can be served with Mexican entrées or in breakfast tacos.

FRUIT AND FRUIT JUICES   ◆   Most fruit should be eaten whole and raw. Fresh fruit is an excellent source of vitamin C, but that's destroyed during canning or bottling. Other phytonutrients, such as vitamin A and minerals, are retained in canned fruit and fruit juices. Fresh juices, on the other hand, retain vitamins, minerals, and phytonutrients because the only part that's removed is the fiber. They can be a good way to get condensed nutrients, but remember that the fiber in whole fruit has many important health benefits and slows down fruit sugar absorption. A few cans of mandarin oranges and pineapple are good to have on hand to add to salads and some entrées.

JAMS AND SWEETENERS   ◆   High-quality jam will list fruit as its first ingredient. It costs more, but you get better nutritional value for your money and it takes less of the product to satisfy. In choosing syrup, be sure to buy real maple syrup instead of the variety sweetened with corn syrup. The taste of natural maple syrup is wonderful and you'll use less of it. Top whole-grain pancakes and waffles with fat-free sour cream and fresh fruit make a wonderful weekend breakfast. Sprinkle ground cinnamon on the topping for added nutritional value.

OIL, VINEGAR, AND NUT BUTTERS • Healthy oils have gained new respect in nutrition circles. The best oils to use are those high in omega-3 fatty acids such as flaxseed (not for cooking), macadamia nut, organic extra virgin olive, organic walnut, and canola pressed from rapeseeds that haven't been genetically modified. Give rice-bran oil a try, too. Scientists at Louisiana State University found that it lowers overall cholesterol and low-density lipoprotein cholesterol more effectively than fiber does.

Nut butters offer all the phytonutrients and healthy oils found in whole nuts and are more digestible. Look for brands that have little or no salt added. Use nut butters in place of butter or other spreads to increase the nutrient value of whole-grain bread products. Sesame butter, for example, makes wonderful salad dressings and is a component of the popular spread hummous.

Vinegar is available in varying degrees of acidity. Using balsamic low-acid vinegar to dress salads will also cut down on the amount you need to use.

BEVERAGES OTHER THAN FRUIT JUICES • Green tea has many health benefits and is an excellent beverage to have on hand. Black and herbal teas are increasing popular, and now most coffeehouses offer chai as an alternative to coffee, plus you can find many good flavors to enjoy at home. You do need to keep in mind that most chai products contain sugar, so enjoy them occasionally, but not daily. Coffee is a complex substance with more than three hundred different chemicals in it. Even decaffeinated coffee contains most of them, some with impressive health benefits. Coffee drinkers were happy to find that a recent Harvard University study reported that coffee drinking might reduce the incidence of Parkinson's disease, particularly in men. Apparently use of postmenopausal estrogens negated the same potential benefit for women. Other studies have highlighted the negative effect of caffeine for those with heart arrhythmias (irregular heartbeats). If you enjoy coffee, consider switching to an organic brand and always buy water-processed decaffeinated coffee to avoid the chemicals used in caffeine removal.

The health benefits of drinking wine are legend, but many wines contain residues of pesticides and insecticides that make it impossible for all to enjoy them. The addition of sulfites is another practice that can create problems for many consumers. One way to overcome such reactions is to buy organic wines, which are made from grapes raised without the use of chemicals and contain significantly lower levels of sulfites.

A WORD ABOUT ORGANIC WINES • Agricultural methods that have stripped soil of minerals essential in our food have had the same effect on wine production. As a result, grapes are one of the most heavily sprayed crops.

Spraying pesticides on vines and applying them to roots results in chemical residue in wine after the grapes are crushed. Some of these chemicals are cause for concern and account for many adverse reactions people experience from drinking wine.

Organic vintners fertilize with composted animal manure and promote biodiversity by planting cover crops. These crops in turn attract beneficial insects, spiders, and predatory mites that replace chemical pesticides and insecticides. Instead of spraying weeds with herbicides, organic vintners mow weeds to the ground and allow them to compost naturally. The more mature European organic wine industry consistently captures top honors among the world's top ten wines. California, with its robust wine business, leads our nation in organic wine production.

Smaller amounts of cultured yeast are used in organic wines because wild yeast remains in the crush to aid fermentation. Perhaps one of the most important aspects of organic wine production is the lessened use of sulfur dioxide as an antioxidant, no doubt because of the higher presence of natural antioxidants.

The U.S. Department of Agriculture has recently defined how organic wines are to be labeled. Organic wine must now be made from organically grown grapes and *without any added sulfites*. Most wines that have been sold as organic must now be labeled as made from organic grapes, because they contain small amounts of sulfites added for stability. Conventional wines typically contain two to three times more sulfites than organically grown wines. Labeling wines as "Certified Organically Grown" distinguishes them from conventional wines. Organic wines are still good dollar values since they have not yet captured sufficient consumer attention to command premium prices.

CHAPTER SIX

Step Three: Fix Your Meals

THE 7-COLOR CUISINE PLAN is unique in two ways. First, it uses a modular design to create a mental picture of what constitutes daily meal plans. Second, weekly meal plans, shopping lists, and recipes are grouped together in a week-at-a-glance format that follows the guidelines presented in the first two steps, get set and go shopping.

Daily Menu Modules

Busy people love the modular approach because they can easily design meals that feature the beauty of fresh fruit and vegetables. All you have to think about is what goes into each module and how they're assembled to create meals that are a feast for the eyes and comforting for the soul. Salads and vegetable side dishes are key components for midday and evening meals, while fruit makes up the breakfast core. Snacks include fruit, vegetables, and nuts. Even good, dark chocolate has its place in 7-Color Cuisine. In this system, whole grains and legumes occupy another important niche, while animal foods play supporting roles. This is a different way of thinking about meals than most of us are used to, and that's why you push your shopping cart toward the produce section first. Let's begin with the simplest and most overlooked part of meals with ingredients found in the produce section.

Super Salad Savvy

Salads are extremely versatile, and you can combine a nearly limitless variety of fruit and vegetables into main course, lunch, and dinner salads. Super Salads are appealing to the senses and contain at least four choices from your daily color palette. What may surprise you is the significant protein content of Super Salads. Each derives between 5 and 10 percent of its calories from protein—even salads that contain fruit, which does not contain protein—because the salads contain a significant amount of greens.

Super Salads can be made in just a few minutes by using the following four-module plan. You'll need to have the components of each module ready to use. Daily menu plans list the ingredients you'll need to purchase and, with the help of the pantry management lists in Appendix C, you'll have everything ready to go. This saves tremendous time and is the only way busy people can enjoy nutritious meals without spending hours in the kitchen.

Super Salads are not "super-sized." Restaurants that offer salad bars make two important mistakes. First, the salad plates are too large. A properly balanced Super Salad uses a seven-inch plate, not a dinner-sized plate. Second, salad dressings are served with a ladle. Many customers are really after the dressing. A well-balanced Super Salad is so rich in flavor it requires little dressing.

Module One

Shop for the freshest salad greens, selecting organic whenever possible. Look for loose-leaf lettuce in any of several varieties, including green and red romaine, red leaf, oak leaf, butter head,

A NEW WAY OF EATING

Bibb, chicory (Belgian endive), watercress, and frisée. You can use any of these alone or combined. Mixes of several of these lettuces can be found in bulk or packaged baby green mixes, which often also include bok choy, mizuna, curly endive, tatsoi, kale, radicchio, arugula, watercress, and red and green mustard. These will be found at local farmers' markets, where the composition varies depending on the season. Supermarkets offer packages of mixed greens with a more standard mix of greens. You will find them labeled as mesclun, baby greens, or salad mix. Bags of theme-mixed greens with fresh herbs—Italian, for example—can also be found.

It is best to use the mixes within a day or two of purchase, but they will last four or five days if you gently wash and dry them on paper towels right after bringing them home. When slightly dry, roll the leaves in layers of paper towels and refrigerate them in a plastic produce bag. Spinach, radicchio, Belgian endive, whole green herbs such as basil, and shredded red and green cabbage can also be used in this module.

Place 2 cups of green, red, or purple leaves torn into bite-sized pieces on a salad plate. You may also use a leaf or two of whole lettuce or other greens for a decorative effect.

Module Two

Vegetables and fruit that you place on the greens make up the second layer. Choose what's available locally and organically grown whenever possible. You'll see that some salad combinations in this book feature tropical fruit, including pineapple, mangoes, papaya, paw-paw, passion fruit, and bananas. For most people, these are not local, but they are available year-round and close to the time they were harvested. Seasonal salads not only provide interest, but also fruit and vegetables at the peak of their ripeness. Tropical salads make great accompaniments to main course soups.

Summer salads feature fresh, crisp vegetables. This is the time of year when you can make delicious salads from several kinds of tomatoes, including heritage varieties now making a comeback. These tomatoes are multicolored, juicy, and sweet. Many kinds of cherry tomatoes are also available, including those in unusual shapes and colors such as yellow and orange. These other colors have different flavors than red tomatoes because the colors are different sets of phytonutrient pigments. You may like some of them better than the red tomato taste you've become accustomed to, and, at the very least, they add interest, variety, and additional protective nutrients.

Cucumbers are another summer commodity available in several burpless varieties. Most are long and slender with soft skins that should be left on the fruit. Round lemon cucumbers are a special treat, although they may be hard to find. You can marinate any of the summer cucumbers in a mixture of yogurt or fat-free sour cream, vinegar, dill weed, and pepper.

Sweet bell peppers and hot peppers come in shades of red, yellow, orange, green, white, and purple. Spicy peppers are always found in salsas, and you will find several recipes for these. One version uses tomatillos, a small, husk-covered, green fruit from the tomato family. Other vegetables plentiful in summer are sugar snap peas, green beans, artichoke hearts, shredded carrots, beets, fresh corn, radishes, daikon, sweet onions, fresh basil, and parsley.

Winter salads typically feature many varieties of citrus fruit (oranges, blood oranges, mandarins, tangerines, and grapefruit) and avocados. Shredded daikon, a long, white, mild radish, adds a nice touch to citrus salads. Several varieties of pears and apples and wilted spinach or shredded cabbage are also good choices for cooler weather salads. Cilantro and arugula (also called *rocket*) are plentiful during winter months in many areas. A rocket salad is a good choice during the winter months because it warms you with its spiciness. Cilantro is always a good choice with fruit. You can also enjoy a mental trip to the tropics as suggested above with salads made from pineapple, mango, papaya, bananas, plantains, and kiwi.

As the seasons change, additional fruits and vegetables such as asparagus and pomegranates can be added for variety. This module is where you use your creativity, making up new and interesting combinations. It is fun to come up with your own creations. Use a total of 1 cup of fruit or vegetables in Module Two.

Module Three

Using creative toppings is the next step in salad savvy. Crumbled cheese, sliced or whole nuts, soy nuts, dried fruit, seeds, chopped herbs, shredded unsweetened coconut, beans, and whole grain croutons are great toppings. Depending on how you arrange the fruit and vegetables, you can place the toppings along one side. For example, if you alternate slices of avocado and orange segments, you might place slices of fresh strawberries or other berries at the top of the arrangement. Dried fruits and nuts make a good third module. Cherries, cranberries, and raisins are a welcome addition to any salads, and you can mix and match fruit and vegetables to suit your preference. Sunflower seeds, sesame seeds, pine nuts, almonds, or broken bits of organic walnuts and organic pecans add interest and taste. It takes so little time to build these lovely creations, and you feed your soul while you're making them. Use ⅛ to ¼ cup of toppings. Nuts and crumbled cheese are nutrient dense, so use ⅛ cup of those. Croutons, beans, bottled peppers, capers, olives, and dried fruit are lower in fat, so ¼ cup is an appropriate amount.

TABLE 6-1   *Salad Savvy Module Suggestions*

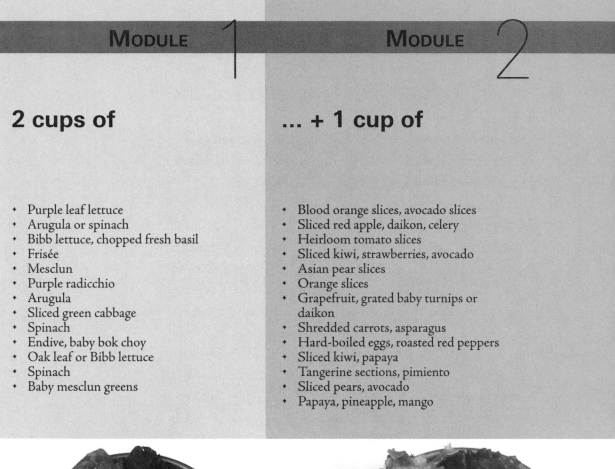

MODULE 1	MODULE 2
2 cups of	**... + 1 cup of**
• Purple leaf lettuce	• Blood orange slices, avocado slices
• Arugula or spinach	• Sliced red apple, daikon, celery
• Bibb lettuce, chopped fresh basil	• Heirloom tomato slices
• Frisée	• Sliced kiwi, strawberries, avocado
• Mesclun	• Asian pear slices
• Purple radicchio	• Orange slices
• Arugula	• Grapefruit, grated baby turnips or daikon
• Sliced green cabbage	• Shredded carrots, asparagus
• Spinach	• Hard-boiled eggs, roasted red peppers
• Endive, baby bok choy	• Sliced kiwi, papaya
• Oak leaf or Bibb lettuce	• Tangerine sections, pimiento
• Spinach	• Sliced pears, avocado
• Baby mesclun greens	• Papaya, pineapple, mango

A NEW WAY OF EATING

MODULE 3

... + 1/8 cup of nuts or cheese, plus 1/4 cup croutons

+ Sliced almonds
+ Broken organic pecan pieces, bleu cheese
+ Goat cheese or fresh mozzarella
+ Pine nuts
+ Pomegranate seeds
+ Organic pecans, feta cheese
+ Tamari sunflower seeds
+ Sesame seeds
+ Celery and sesame seeds, rye bread croutons
+ Toasted soy nuts
+ Organic walnuts
+ Poppy seeds, dried cherries or cranberries
+ Blueberries, coconut

MODULE 4

... + 1 tablespoon of

+ Balsamic vinaigrette
+ Ranch dressing
+ Lemon olive oil, white wine vinegar, pepper
+ Lime juice, macadamia nut oil
+ Lemon juice, sesame oil
+ Creamy Caesar
+ Rice bran wine vinaigrette
+ Spicy miso dressing
+ Warm bacon dressing
+ Red wine vinaigrette
+ Organic walnut oil, lemon juice
+ Creamy ginger dressing
+ Raspberry vinaigrette

Module Four

Now is the time to crown your creation with a dressing. The greens and vegetables or fruit are so flavorful that you need only 1 tablespoon of a good oil or dressing. Nut and flavored oils are excellent as dressings: macadamia nut, organic walnut, sesame (untoasted), avocado, lemon, basil, garlic-, lemon- or pepper-infused olive oil and a little vinegar, lemon, or lime juice. Buy the best oils and vinegar and use them sparingly. You can also use premixed dressings, but be sure they don't contain a lot of sugar and salt. Read the labels and ingredient list carefully and evaluate the product according to the label tips in Appendix B. More unusual dressings to look for are miso- and yogurt-based dressings. Ranch or creamy cheese dressings can be great, as is raspberry vinaigrette. Because you'll be using only 1 tablespoon, you can choose from a wide variety of dressings to add zest and interest to your Super Salads.

She Hated Salads

Janet is a professional woman who shares her home with her aging parents. Her mother is a fabulous cook, and she always serves a large family-style salad that contains lots of goodies at dinner. Janet confided in me that she hates to upset her mom, but she really dislikes these salads. A lot of it had to do with facing an intimidating bowl of crunchy stuff. Janet was turned off by the whole tossed salad idea, especially because the salad dressing covered whatever else was being served in the bowl. I showed Janet how to prepare really creative personalized salads using Super Salad Savvy. She now enjoys fixing her own attractive salads and shares her creations with her parents. They're all enjoying this new approach to one of their favorite parts of the meal. Is there someone in your house who dislikes salads? The appeal of small, attractive plates of salad that turned Janet into a salad lover may be the answer.

Any of these salads can make a satisfying lunch or main meal, especially if you add protein such as cottage cheese, beans, marinated tofu, hard-boiled eggs, or flaked fish. Table 6-1 summarizes salad combinations. You'll find recipes for others in the next part of *7-Color Cuisine*.

Sample Shopping List (weekly amounts per person)

Module One
Greens (½ pound assorted from the following choices)

+ arugula
+ cabbage, purple and green
+ colored "greens," including Belgian endive, radicchio, hearts of palm
+ leaf lettuce
+ mesclun
+ spinach

Module Two
Fruits and vegetables (7 cups from the following choices)

+ apple
+ avocados
+ blood oranges
+ blueberries (frozen berries are okay)
+ grapefruit
+ kiwi
+ lemons
+ limes
+ mango

- oranges
- papaya
- pears
- pineapple
- strawberries
- tangerines
- asparagus
- bell peppers (assorted colors)
- carrots
- celery
- cucumber
- daikon
- heirloom tomatoes

MODULE THREE

Nuts and Seeds (¾ cup of any of the following)
- almonds, sliced
- coconut (unsweetened and shredded)
- organic pecans
- pine nuts
- poppy seeds
- rye bread (sliced to toast and crumbled)
- sesame seeds
- soy nuts
- tamari sunflower seeds
- organic walnuts

Cheese (⅛ cup of any of the following)
- feta cheese
- goat cheese
- mozzarella (fresh)

Dried Fruit (3 cups of any of the following)

+ cherries
+ cranberries
+ raisins

Croutons (¼ cup total)

+ croutons
+ beans

Condiments (¼ cup of any of the following)

+ capers
+ olives
+ pimientos
+ roasted red peppers

MODULE FOUR

Dressings (Organic Oils, Vinegars, and Other Dressings)*

+ bacon dressing
+ balsamic vinaigrette
+ balsamic vinegar
+ creamy Caesar, ginger, and ranch dressings
+ macadamia nut oil
+ organic olive oil, extra virgin
+ raspberry vinaigrette
+ red wine vinaigrette
+ red wine vinegar
+ rice wine vinegar
+ sesame oil
+ spicy miso dressing
+ organic walnut oil
+ white wine vinegar

NOTE: *Most ready-made dressings will be in the refrigerated section of the store. These don't contain preservatives. Choose those without sweeteners if possible. You can easily use your own oil and vinegar dressings for any of these salads using the ingredients listed above.*

---

* Oil and vinegar from cruets: Use 1 tablespoon of the oil and ½ tablespoon of the vinegar.

Herbs and Spices

- celery seed
- cinnamon
- fresh green herbs, including basil, parsley, cilantro, tarragon, and peppermint
- nutmeg
- peppercorns (multicolor to grind)

Add as much and as many of these as you want. Fresh basil and peppermint are often used in Module One to lend special character to a salad.

Nutrition Savvy • Purchase a bottle of liquid vitamin E oil at a natural foods store and squirt a dropper-full atop organic oils to maintain optimal freshness before storing them. You'll need to refrigerate good organic vinegar, including balsamic, after opening because otherwise they'll grow mold and spoil, especially in warmer climates.

Main Course Magic

Planning dinners in *7-Color Cuisine* is simplified with two basic designs: the entrée plan and the main course plan. The entrée and main course in these plans supply a substantial amount of

TABLE 6-2 *Summary of Entrée Plan and Main Course Plan*

Entrée	Main Course
Fish, poultry, meat loaf (meat or legume)	Soup, stew, casserole, stir fry, vegetarian pizza, quiche
Vegetable side dish	
Whole-grain side dish	Super Salad
Super Salad	

protein for the day. The entrée plan contains four components: an entrée and three side dishes (a vegetable, a grain, and a Super Salad). In some recipes, the entrée is served on top of either the grain or vegetable, instead of serving one of them as a side dish. Main courses are more complex and contain protein-rich components, whole-grain rice or pasta, and vegetables. All main course recipes are served with a Super Salad. Table 6-2 summarizes the two plans.

The entrée plan is a classic meal, similar to what you would order in a restaurant. Once you begin working with the plan at home, you'll find it easier to order more healthy selections from a menu. This is the plan you'd follow when planning a meal around a barbecue or when cooking something special for guests. Keep in mind that the serving sizes are small, so although the plan seems to contain a lot of food, it is well balanced nutritionally.

The main course plan is the model for many family favorites, and its leftovers make great lunches or breakfasts the next day. Main course recipes in *7-Color Cuisine* emphasize ideal proportions among vegetables, protein foods, and rice or pasta. You'll develop a good sense of how to adjust old family favorites to make them more nutritious. The main course plan will also show you how to modify ready-to-eat items like take-home pizza to balance nutrition. Recipes for both plans offered in this book emphasize color and an optimum balance of protein, carbohydrate, and fat. Examples of the two plans follow, with recipes to complete the color palette for each meal.

The Classic Entrée Plan
Macadamia nut oil has become a favorite of mine, although I also use organic olive oil from local growers and organic salt-free but-

ter, depending on the recipe. Macadamia nut oil from Australia is unfiltered and unprocessed and works well as a substitute for butter. Macadamia nut oil contains no transfats and only 2 grams of saturated fat; it's higher in monounsaturated fats than other oils and richer in healthy omega-3 fatty acids. (For metric conversions, refer to the metric conversion table in Appendix F.) It's an excellent cooking and baking oil that can be heated to the high temperatures used in stir frying without damaging oil molecules. The following entrée features chopped macadamia nuts and oil.

Macadamia Nut–Encrusted Cod

SEASON
Any

SERVINGS
4 (4 ounces cod each)

PREPARATION TIME
40 minutes
(25 minutes baking)

NOTE: *Steam the spinach, arugula, or other dark greens as little as possible, just enough to "subdue" them. Lightly wilted greens will retain all of their nutrients, are tastier, and look nicer.*

INGREDIENTS

- **1 pound cod or other firm white fish (or skinned and boned chicken breast)**
- **2/3 cup bread crumbs (unseasoned whole-grain)**
- **1/3 cup macadamia nuts, chopped**
- **1 egg, beaten with 1 teaspoon water**
- **1/4 cup flat, Italian parsley, chopped**
- **1 tablespoon macadamia nut oil**
- **4 cups spinach or arugula, lightly wilted**
- **1 tablespoon macadamia nut oil**

DIRECTIONS

1. Wash and pat cod dry.
2. Combine breadcrumbs, macadamia nuts, and half the parsley.
3. Cut cod into four pieces and dip in the egg-and-water mixture, then in seasoned breadcrumbs.
4. Place cod in a shallow baking dish so that the pieces are close together. Sprinkle with remaining parsley.
5. Drizzle oil on top.
6. Bake uncovered approximately 25 minutes in a 375°F oven until browned and crusty. If you substitute chicken in this recipe, you'll need to cover the dish to retain moisture; bake 40 minutes at 350°F. Remove the cover during the last 10 minutes of baking to brown the crust.
7. Serve over a bed (1 cup) of lightly wilted spinach or arugula.

Take a moment to study the nutrition facts for this recipe, contained in Table 6-3, because you'll see how serving an entrée over a vegetable improves a meal's overall nutrition. This is one important method you can use to improve foods that have less than optimal nutritional profiles. Check the information below the table to see if your observations are correct.

CALORIES ◆ The small addition of spinach adds slightly to the total number of calories, but the entrée also contains more nutrients. The spinach also adds a brilliant green and pleasing moisture and flavor.

TOTAL FAT AND SATURATED FATS ◆ Although macadamia nuts and oil are high in total fat, they are low in saturated fats. Macadamia nuts contain 3.5 grams of saturated fat per ¼ cup serving and a whopping 17 grams of healthy monounsaturated fats. Macadamia nut oil contains 2 grams of saturated fat and 11 grams of monounsaturated fats per tablespoon, about the same as organic extra virgin olive oil and more than canola oil.

TABLE 6-3 *Nutrition Facts for Cod and Spinach*

Nutrition Facts	Cod	Spinach
Calories	304	52
Total fat	13.7 grams	0.5 gram
Saturated fat	2.1 grams	0
Cholesterol	106 milligrams	0
Sodium	275 milligrams	126 milligrams
Carbohydrates	14.8 grams	6.8 grams
Fiber	1.4 grams	4.3 grams
Protein	30.7 grams	5.3 grams

A NEW WAY OF EATING

CHOLESTEROL ✦ Animal products are the only source of cholesterol. Consequently, adding spinach adds more nutrients without adding cholesterol.

SODIUM ✦ Saltwater fish naturally contain sodium, and none is added in this recipe. Spinach contains sodium also, but it contains seven times more potassium to balance the salt. Spinach also provides magnesium and trace minerals, including iron, manganese, zinc, and copper.

CARBOHYDRATES AND FIBER ✦ This is a low-carbohydrate recipe in which breadcrumbs supply most of the carbohydrates. Spinach or other dark greens are relatively low in carbohydrates, but high in fiber. Adding green vegetables to entrées can improve fiber content considerably.

PROTEIN ✦ The entrée provides most of the protein for the meal, but spinach (or arugula) contributes a substantial amount as well.

The colors represented in this meal so far are white (cod and egg), tan (bread crumbs and nuts), condiments (oil), and green (spinach). We need to complete the color palette now with side dishes. Let's begin with a Super Salad, because that's the simplest way to balance colors.

This elegant meal contains 615 calories, 30.2 total grams of fat, 4.3 grams of saturated fat, 106 milligrams of cholesterol, 325 milligrams of sodium, 50.6 grams of carbohydrate, 9.4 grams of fiber, and 34.6 grams of protein.

This dinner contains six out of seven colors and accounts for 31 percent of a 2,000-calorie daily intake or 41 percent of a 1,500-calorie anti-aging regimen. It is relatively high in total fat, but it's healthy fat. The meal is low in cholesterol and

Blackberry and Pear Salad with Lime Ginger Dressing

SEASON
Any as long as berries and pears are available

SERVINGS
1 (standard size for Super Salads)

PREPARATION TIME
10 minutes

NUTRITION FACTS FOR SALAD AND DRESSING
calories 237
total fat 14.3 grams
saturated fat 1.8 grams
cholesterol 0 milligrams
sodium 35 milligrams
carbohydrate 24.4 grams
fiber 7.1 grams
protein 2.5 grams

SERVING SIZE
1 tablespoon

NOTE: *Rounding out this dinner is 1 cup steamed brown rice.*

Salad

INGREDIENTS

- **2 cups purple leaf lettuce, torn into bite-sized pieces**
- **½ cup golden pears, seeded and sliced lengthwise**
- **½ cup blackberries, fresh**
- **1 tablespoon sunflower seeds**
- **1 tablespoon ginger, candied**

DIRECTIONS

1. Arrange pear slices in a fan shape over lettuce.

2. Place berries at base of the fan and sprinkle candied ginger and sunflower seeds on top.

3. Add lime ginger dressing (recipe follows).

Lime Ginger Dressing

INGREDIENTS

- **½ cup macadamia nut oil**
- **¼ cup lime juice, freshly squeezed**
- **¼ cup cilantro, chopped**
- **1 teaspoon fresh ginger root, peeled and grated**
- **½ teaspoon seasoned salt**

DIRECTIONS

Mix the ingredients and chill before serving.

Steamed Brown Rice

SERVINGS
2 (1 cup per serving)

PREPARATION TIME
55 minutes

NUTRITION FACTS

calories	219
total fat	1.8 grams
saturated fat	0.4 grams
cholesterol	0 milligrams
sodium	355 milligrams
carbohydrate	45.3 grams
fiber	3.5 grams
protein	5.5 grams

INGREDIENTS

1 cup brown rice, long-grain

2 cups water

1 teaspoon fat-free chicken broth

1 tablespoon scallions, minced

1 teaspoon thyme, fresh (or ½ teaspoon dried)

DIRECTIONS

1. Bring water to a boil.

2. Wash rice and drain.

3. Add chicken broth.

4. Add rice, scallions, and thyme.

5. Cover with a snug-fitting lid and steam 45 minutes.

6. Fluff with a fork before serving

sodium. Protein content is high, and complex carbohydrates with fiber are moderate. What color is missing? Include it in another meal.

Main Course Plan

Soups offer ideal combinations of ingredients that support one another with color and flavor. Many vegetables release their phytonutrients into the soup base when they're cooked, and this makes a rich and nutritious meal that's easy to digest. Soups can be enjoyed either hot during cold winter months or cold during warmer weather.

The following soup recipes make up a colorful palette of red, orange, yellow, green, purple, tan, and creamy white, the seven colors of the 7-Color system. This makes it easy to complete a meal with complementary colors in a Super Salad. Crusty artisan bread completes each meal. The soups are all high in protein, much derived from legumes. The red, orange, yellow, and green soups are especially tasty when puréed and topped with fat-free sour cream or yogurt. The creamy white, purple, and tan soups are more appealing when prepared as hearty, chunky soups.

Pressure cooking is a great way to prepare these soups. The flavors blend wonderfully, bright colors are retained, and cooking time is a mere 15 minutes at 8 pounds per square inch (psi). This makes it easy for busy people to enjoy them anytime. Several colored soups can be prepared in one afternoon and frozen for later use.

Three of the soups presented here appear in the four-week daily menu plans: Lentils with Canadian Bacon, Ginger Orange, and Purple Borscht with Beef. The other soups in this section can be substituted for any main course in the menu plans. Table 6-4 shows the modules that make up 7-Color soups.

TABLE 6-4 *7-Color Soup Modules*

Color Soup	Oil (2 Tbsp.)	Base or Broth (4 cups)	Vegetables (6 cups)	Protein (1 cup)	Spice(s)
Red Hungarian	Macadamia nut	Vegetable base or broth (water with 1 Tbsp. soup base)	Red onion, beets, beet and red chard stalks, red pepper, tomatoes	Red lentils	Hungarian paprika
Yellow Curry	Macadamia nut	Vegetable base or broth (water with 1 Tbsp. soup base)	Yellow onion, garlic, yellow squash, yellow bell pepper	Yellow split peas	Sweet curry powder
Ginger Orange	Macadamia nut	Vegetable base or broth (water with 1 Tbsp. soup base)	Yellow onion, sweet potato, rutabaga, carrots, orange bell pepper, tomato	Red lentils	Grated fresh ginger, cinnamon, parsley
Zesty Green	Macadamia nut or extra virgin olive	Vegetable or chicken base or broth (water with 1 Tbsp. soup base)	Scallion tops, kale, asparagus, spinach, parsley	French green lentils	Tarragon, nutmeg, lime zest
Winter White	Macadamia nut or organic walnut	Vegetable or chicken base or broth (water with 1 Tbsp. soup base)	Leeks, garlic, cauliflower, turnip, parsnips, bok choy	Organic northern white beans	White pepper, cardamom, coriander
Purple Borscht with Beef	Extra virgin olive	Vegetable or beef base or broth (water with 1 Tbsp. soup base)	Purple onion, turnip, parsnip, russet potato, carrots, beets, purple cabbage, tomato	1 cup beef cubes or brown lentils	Vinegar, pepper, chives
Lentils with Canadian Bacon	Macadamia nut or extra virgin olive	Vegetable or ham base (water with 1 Tbsp. soup base)	Red onions, carrots, celery, green, yellow and red peppers	Brown lentils, Canadian bacon	Parsley, pepper
7-Color Minestrone	Macadamia nut or extra virgin olive	Vegetable or beef base (water with 1 Tbsp. soup base)	Leek, yellow onion, garlic, carrots, green pepper, zucchini, green beans, tomatoes, purple cabbage	Cannellini beans, Parmesan cheese	Basil, oregano, thyme, French sorrel

Hungarian Red Soup

SEASON
Winter

SERVINGS
4 (2 cups each)

PREPARATION TIME
20 minutes

COOKING TIME
1 hour

NUTRITION FACTS

calories	294
total fat	8.4 grams
saturated fat	1.1 grams
cholesterol	0 milligrams
sodium	612 milligrams
carbohydrate	40.2 grams
fiber	8.3 grams
protein	14.9 grams

NOTE: *This soup recipe and several others were contributed by Gayle Pruitt, nutritionist at MacNut Oil Company, a distributor of an excellent brand of macadamia nut oil from Australia.*

This is a zesty soup, perfect for cold winter evenings when beets and chard are at peak sweetness with highest nutrient content. It's paired in the dinner menu plan with a salad made from kiwi, oranges, Belgian endive, and spinach, and served with a crusty, whole-grain artisan bread to dip in the soup, if this appeals to you. Red antioxidants help improve circulation to the extremities and provide some of our best defenses against cold weather by maintaining bodily warmth.

INGREDIENTS

- 2 tablespoons macadamia nut oil
- 1 medium red onion, finely chopped (approximately 1 cup)
- 1 cup red lentils
- 1 beet plus beet stalks (not leaves), cut into 1-inch cubes (1 cup)
- 1 bunch red chard stalks (reserve leaves), chopped (3 cups)
- 1 red pepper, cut into 1-inch cubes (1 cup)

- 1 tablespoon prepackaged vegetable soup base dissolved in 1 quart warm water or 1 quart of low-fat, low-salt vegetable broth
- 1 can fire-roasted and diced tomatoes (14.5 ounces)
- Hungarian paprika (approximately 3 teaspoons)
- Sour cream or yogurt, fat-free (1 tablespoon per serving)

DIRECTIONS

NOTE: *We complete the palette for this meal with a tricolor green salad with oranges, kiwi, and pistachio nuts.*

NOTE: *The reserved chard leaves can be combined with butternut squash for a lutein-rich vegetable side dish.*

1. Sauté onion with oil until translucent.

2. Add lentils, beets, chard and beet stalks, and red pepper cubes.

3. Cook for another 3 or 4 minutes.

4. Add soup base or vegetable broth and simmer 40 minutes or until beets and lentils are done.

5. Add diced tomatoes and paprika. The heat of Hungarian paprika varies, so be sure to flavor to your taste. (Penzey's Hungarian half-sharp paprika is wonderful, but quite hot.)

6. Cook an additional 5 minutes.

7. After the soup has cooked, place in a blender or food processor and purée. Add vegetable broth until soup has a velvety texture. A good blender or food processor is needed to purée this soup.

8. Add 1 tablespoon of fat-free sour cream or yogurt to each serving.

Belgian Endive, Kiwi, and Orange Salad

SERVINGS
2 (Super Salad modules)

PREPARATION TIME
10 minutes

NUTRITION FACTS

calories	266
total fat	10.3 grams
saturated fat	1.2 grams
cholesterol	0 milligrams
sodium	153 milligrams
carbohydrate	37.9 grams
fiber	9.2 grams
protein	5.5 grams

INGREDIENTS

4 cups combination Belgian endive, purple radicchio, and baby spinach

1 cup kiwi, peeled and sliced

1 cup orange segments

¼ cup raw pistachio nuts, shelled

2 tablespoons balsamic vinaigrette

DIRECTIONS

1. Divide greens and radicchio between two salad plates.

2. Top plates with fruit.

3. Add pistachio nuts and dressing.

Yellow Curry Soup

SEASON
Autumn

SERVINGS
4 (2 cups each)

PREPARATION TIME
1 hour, 15 minutes

NUTRITION FACTS
calories 288
fat 7.8 grams
saturated fat 1 gram
cholesterol 0 milligrams
sodium 535 milligrams
carbohydrate 39.9 grams
fiber 14.8 grams
protein 14.6 grams

This soup, another of Gayle Pruitt's, blends some the best of early autumn produce. Evenings are getting chilly, and the last of the summer and fall produce is being harvested. Curry adds an interesting flavor to the soup. Sweet curry powder contains a large percentage of the brilliant yellow spice turmeric and a nice blend of other antioxidants. Turmeric by itself is not especially flavorful, but it is high in an anti-inflammatory agent known as curcumin. Look for turmeric with at least 5 percent curcumin. As winter approaches, add more deep yellow and orange fruits and vegetables to your menus. The antioxidants from these colors offer protection against winter colds and flu.

INGREDIENTS

- **2 tablespoons macadamia nut oil**
- **1 medium yellow Spanish onion, finely chopped (1 cup)**
- **2 garlic cloves, finely chopped**
- **1 cup of yellow split peas**
- **2 medium yellow squash, chopped fine**
- **1 large yellow bell pepper, chopped fine**
- **1 tablespoon prepackaged vegetable or chicken soup base dissolved in 1 quart water or same amount of fat-free vegetable or chicken broth**
- **2 teaspoons sweet, yellow curry powder or turmeric**

DIRECTIONS

1. Sauté onions in oil until they are translucent.

2. Add garlic and cook another 2 minutes.

3. Add split peas, squash, and bell pepper and sauté an additional 2 minutes.

4. Pour in vegetable broth (or chicken soup base) and curry powder (or turmeric) and cook for 40 minutes or until split peas are done.

5. Purée soup in a food processor.

NOTE: *Edible, fresh squash blossoms are great to top this soup, although they made be scarce during fall months.*

Zesty Green Soup

SEASON
Spring

SERVINGS
4 (2 cups each)

PREPARATION TIME
1 hour, 20 minutes

NUTRITION FACTS
calories 293
fat 8 grams
saturated fat 1.1 grams
cholesterol 0 milligrams
sodium 555 milligrams
carbohydrate 39.5 grams
fiber 16.1 grams
protein 16.3 grams

Spring greens provide wonderful antioxidants that help detoxify the body. They have a slightly pungent taste and offer a nice flavor contrast to golden and creamy white winter soups. The green soup combines several kids of spring vegetables to enhance flavor and provide a greater selection of detoxifying nutrients. In early spring, tarragon is bursting forth with its bright green leaves and adds a nice flavor.

INGREDIENTS

- **2 tablespoons macadamia nut oil**
- **1 cup green onion (scallion), chopped**
- **1½ cup kale (stalks removed), chopped**
- **1 tablespoon vegetarian soup base, dissolved in 1 quart hot water or 1 quart fat-free vegetable stock**
- **4 cups spinach leaves, coarsely chopped**
- **2 cups asparagus (tough ends removed), cut in 1-inch lengths**
- **¼ cup parsley leaves, chopped (stems removed)**
- **1 cup French green lentils**
- **½ cup fresh tarragon leaves, chopped**
- **2 teaspoons nutmeg**
- **low-fat yogurt (1 tablespoon per serving)**
- **2 tablespoons lime zest**

DIRECTIONS

1. Sauté green onions in oil in a pressure cooker or 4-quart pot.

2. Add collard greens or kale and sauté 1 to 2 minutes.

3. Pour in vegetable broth or stock and cook 15 minutes.

4. Add lentils, spinach, asparagus, parsley, tarragon, and nutmeg.

5. Place cover on pressure cooker and process at 8 psi for 15 minutes. Or cover pot and cook for 1 hour.

6. Purée in food processor.

7. Top each serving with 1 tablespoon of low-fat yogurt and sprinkle lime zest on top.

Winter White Soup

SEASON
Winter

SERVINGS
4 (2 cups each)

PREPARATION TIME
20 minutes

COOKING TIME
20 minutes

NUTRITION FACTS
calories 282
fat 7.6 grams
saturated fat 1 gram
cholesterol 0 milligrams
sodium 600 milligrams
carbohydrate 42 grams
fiber 10.2 grams
protein 11.6 grams

The pale color of this soup belies a wonderful creamy rich texture and flavor. It just satisfies the mind and appetite to enjoy a bowl on a cold winter evening. Cardamom gives the soup an exotic, sweet taste and is a great tonic spice when energy is lagging. During warmer weather, it is equally tasty served cold with a sprinkling of fresh, chopped sorrel or tarragon.

INGREDIENTS

2 tablespoons macadamia nut oil

2 large leeks (white part only), chopped

2 cloves garlic, chopped

1 tablespoon soup base dissolved in 1 quart hot water or 1 tablespoon low-fat vegetable broth

1 head cauliflower, separated into florets

1 turnip, peeled and cubed

2 small parsnips, peeled and cubed

1 small bok choy (white part only), chopped

1 can (15 ounces) of organic white beans

1 teaspoon cardamom pods, seeds removed and ground

½ white pepper, freshly ground

DIRECTIONS

1. Sauté leeks in oil until they are translucent.

2. Add garlic and cook another 2 minutes.

3. Add soup base or vegetable broth, cauliflower, turnip, parsnip, and bok choy and cook until the cauliflower is soft.

4. Add beans and cardamom.

5. When beans are thoroughly heated through, purée soup in a food processor.

6. Add freshly ground white pepper before serving.

7-Color Minestrone

SEASON
Summer and fall

SERVINGS
8 (12 ounces each)

PREPARATION TIME
1 hour, 20 minutes

NUTRITION FACTS
calories 181
total fat 5 grams
saturated fat 0.9 grams
cholesterol 2 milligrams
sodium 656 milligrams
carbohydrate 26.7 grams
fiber 5.7 grams
protein 7.1 grams

Minestrone is always a welcome addition to weekly menus. What is especially wonderful about this soup is the never-ending variety of good things you can include in the recipe. Choose the vegetables that are in season and change the entire taste of the soup. It is also delicious made with a little meat, if you prefer a nonvegetarian version. Either way, it is chock full of high-quality protein.

INGREDIENTS

2 tablespoons organic extra virgin olive oil

1 leek with a little bit of the green top, chopped

1 small purple onion, chopped

3–4 garlic cloves, minced

5 baby carrots

1 green bell pepper, chopped

3 baby zucchini, sliced or cut into small pieces

¼ pound green beans, trimmed and cut in 1-inch pieces

3 large tomatoes, chopped (peeled is optional)

1 cup fresh basil leaves, chopped

2 cups arugula leaves, chopped

2 large sprigs fresh oregano, leaves stripped from the stem (or ½ teaspoon dried)

1 large sprig fresh thyme, leaves stripped from the stem (or 1 teaspoon dried)

6 leaves fresh French sorrel, chopped

2 tablespoons beef stock paste or dark miso paste or vegetable stock paste

black pepper, freshly ground (a generous amount)

2 teaspoons sea salt (optional)

1 quart water

2 cups dried whole-wheat elbow macaroni

1 can (15 ounces) organic cannellini beans

2 tablespoons Parmesan, Asiago, or Romano cheese, freshly grated

DIRECTIONS

1. In a 5-quart open kettle, lightly sauté leek, onion, and garlic in oil.

2. Add carrots, bell pepper, tomatoes, basil, arugula, oregano, thyme, sorrel, beef stock paste, black pepper, salt, and water.

3. Cover and simmer at least 1 hour (2 hours if time permits). Longer cooking time blends flavors even more. The soup can also be placed in a slow cooker and simmered on its lowest setting during the day.

4. Twenty minutes before the end of cooking, add the uncooked pasta. Uncover pot and stir frequently to make sure pasta doesn't stick.

5. Just before serving, stir in beans.

6. Ladle into large soup bowls and sprinkle with grated cheese.

Breakfast and Lunch Modules

Breakfast and lunch follow the modular scheme as well. Many people skip breakfast because they don't feel hungry or they're in a rush to get out the door. Recent studies have shown that skipping breakfast contributes to weight gain and may be a factor in high cholesterol. After an overnight fast, it's extremely important to eat a wholesome breakfast that jump-starts your metabolism.

Breakfast Modules

Think of color when planning breakfast. Table 6-5 shows two breakfast modules, A and B, each consisting of three sub-modules: two colors of fruit or vegetables, one of creamy white, and one of tan. An additional tan item may be provided in some recipes; this could be flaxseed added to a breakfast shake, or nut butter spread on a whole-grain bread item.

MODULE A

Fruit and Vegetables • Choosing whole fruit or vegetables rich in fiber is preferable to drinking juice. In the breakfast modules, at least one of the fruit or vegetable servings should be eaten whole. In Module A, one of the fruits is added to a blender shake along with yogurt and whey protein powder. The second choice might

TABLE 6-5 *Breakfast Modules*

Module	
A	**B**
2 fruits or vegetables or a combination	2 fruits or vegetables or a combination
Yogurt, milk, or soy milk and whey protein powder	Eggs, yogurt, or cottage cheese
1 whole-grain cereal or bread item	1 whole-grain bread item

be a serving of whole fruit or vegetables eaten on the side or juice added to the blender. Good suggestions are berries, banana, orange, grapefruit, cranberry, papaya, grape, and vegetable juice. Buy fresh or bottled fruit juices, preferably organic, that are low in salt and added sugar. Avoid canned juices.

Dairy and Whey Protein · Whey protein powder provides high-quality protein to a delicious fruity shake for a quick weekday morning breakfast. Another morning option uses yogurt or milk on top of cereal.

Whole-Grain Cereals, Breads, Seeds, and Nuts · Whole grains, seeds, and nuts round out the meal. One option is to choose whole-grain, unsweetened cereal or granola instead of a breakfast shake. Watch out for added oil and sweeteners in granola mixes. The other option is a slice of whole-grain bread, a bagel, or a muffin topped with nut butter such as peanut, almond, organic cashew, or sesame. Hummus makes a great spread as well. These butters and spreads are excellent sources of added protein.

Lunch Modules
The plan includes three lunch modules:
* sandwich pockets
* entrées or main courses from the previous night's dinner
* Super Salads

Each choice fills in the color palette for the day and is high in vegetable protein and fiber. Keeping protein intake high in the middle of the day helps sustain sharp focus and mental concentration. Table 6-6 summarizes the lunch modules.

TABLE 6-6   *Lunch Modules*

Sandwich Module	Dinner Modules	Super Salads

SANDWICH POCKETS MODULES ◆ Avoid the traditional sandwich with two slices of bread because the protein-to-carbohydrate ratio is too low. Pita pockets can hold a lot of greens, sprouts, legumes, and other goodies. In addition, pita pockets are moist and tasty and don't need as much added spread such as mayonnaise.

ENTRÉES OR DINNER MODULES ◆ The leftover dinner module is convenient because many main course options in dinner menus will have more servings than can be eaten in one meal. These make nourishing and quick lunches the next day. For larger appetites and physically active people, add a small Super Salad.

Follow this module also when eating out for lunch; in this case, dinner is actually substituted for lunch. Because a large meal at lunchtime reduces the need for a large dinner, one of the lunch modules replaces dinner. The modular system allows you to interchange meals easily and still maintain an optimal nutritional profile for the day.

SUPER SALADS ◆ Super Salads for lunch can add protein with beans, boiled eggs, cottage cheese, fish, or broiled chicken. During warmer weather, a Super Salad might contain a refreshing assortment of fresh fruit.

Snacks

Snacks are not provided in the menu plans because the meals are well balanced and nutrient-dense. If you need snacks to maintain consistent energy, try healthy alternatives. They include trail mix without added sugar, unsalted nuts, raw sunflower and pumpkin seeds, dried fruit, fresh fruit, baby carrots, raw vegetables with low-fat dip, salsa with low-salt baked chips, hummus, yogurt, low-fat cheese, fat-free granola, plain popcorn, and low-fat/low-sodium whole-grain crackers.

Now that the modules have been explained, it's time to put the first three steps of the 7-Color plan into practice.

Menu Plans, Shopping Lists, and Recipes

The layout of this part of the book is unconventional when compared to many other cookbooks, but it's easier to follow, especially for busy people and those just learning to cook. Plans are organized in the same way that most of us plan and prepare meals. We select a recipe, either entrée or main course, and then decide what to serve with it. Next we make a list, go to the store, and buy the ingredients. When it's time to prepare the meal, we get everything ready and then start cooking. With the *7-Color Cuisine* plan, everything is laid out in weekly menu plans followed by shopping lists and recipes. You can easily change the order of daily menus, if you like, because shopping lists and recipes apply to the entire week.

Most of the recipes are designed for weekdays, when it seems most difficult to eat well. On one weekend day, the plans provide for a larger breakfast and a large evening meal. The other weekend day you may choose to eat out or enjoy a favorite recipe. You might also use this weekend day to experiment with recipes not offered in *7-Color Cuisine,* but which fit into the modular plan.

The Familiar Planner Format: Week and Day at a Glance

Most people use some kind of planner to keep track of daily, weekly, and monthly appointments. The menu plans for *7-Color Cuisine* follow this familiar format and reinforce the importance of careful planning and shopping. The following table illustrates the week-at-a-glance schematic for planning weekly menus around the main meal of the day. Breakfast and lunch menus complete the day's color palette.

Menu Plans

Week at a Glance

Day	Modules	Recipe	Super Salad	Side Dish(es)
1	Entrée			
2	Main course			
3	Entrée			
4	Main course			
5	Entrée			
6	Free			
7	Entrée			

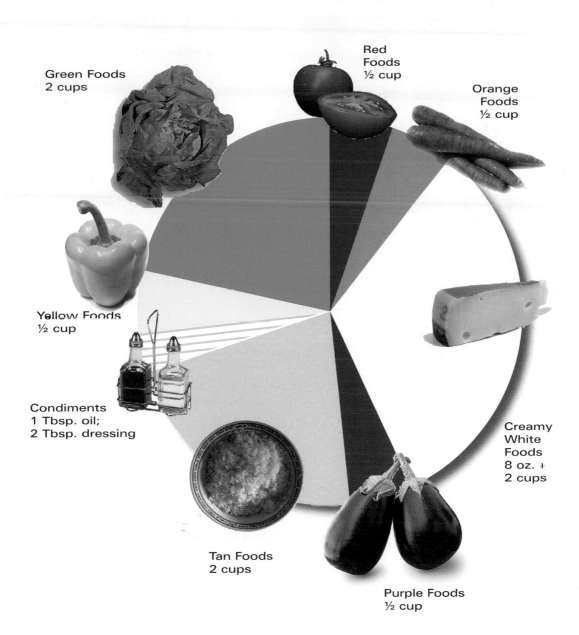

Green Foods
2 cups

Red
Foods
½ cup

Orange
Foods
½ cup

Creamy
White
Foods
8 oz. +
2 cups

Purple Foods
½ cup

Tan Foods
2 cups

Condiments
1 Tbsp. oil;
2 Tbsp. dressing

Yellow Foods
½ cup

FIGURE 3-1 **Amount of Daily Color Consumption**

Whole grains and vegetable pasta are incredibly tasty. Easy to cook, they come in a wide variety of colors and textures and are loaded with healing nutrients.

GET SET—Organic tan foods for the pantry. Clockwise: black and mahogany rice; basmati rice with dried vegetables; wild blend of gourmet brown rice; buckwheat soba noodles, vegetable shells, spinach and chive linguini, and vegetable radiatore.

GO SHOPPING—At the Chico, California, Saturday Farmers' Market, where you can find the freshest, locally grown, in-season, organic (or pesticide-free) produce and so inexpensive! I'm talking with Al Vogel, who is now a farmer, but with whom I team-taught chemistry and biology some years back.

SUPER SALAD SAVV—Module One: Start with 2 cups mixed organic baby greens.

Module Two: Add 1 cup fruit or vegetables (nectarines, oranges).

Module Three: Add quarter cup toppings (nuts, cheese, dried fruit).

Module Four: Add
1 tablespoon dressing
(pomegranate and
blueberry vinaigrette).

FOUR SUPER SALADS. Clockwise: papaya, avocado, cherries, organic baby greens, blue cheese; radicchio shell with cottage cheese, oranges, blackberries, curly endive, walnuts; nectarine, orange, macadamia nuts, organic baby greens; lemon cucumber, purple sweet pepper, mixed tomatoes on frisée. Toppings on the side: sunflower seeds, Gorgonzola cheese, pine nuts, feta cheese with tomato and basil. Dressings: ranch, raspberry vinaigrette, balsamic vinaigrette, lime ginger cilantro.

Dinner—Entrée Plan: Top: pan-seared wild Pacific salmon with tarragon aioli on a bed of fresh basil. Bottom: grilled Chilean sea bass with macadamia nut pesto sauce on a bed of grilled mixed vegetables. Side (top to bottom): green beans with roasted red peppers and almonds; couscous with parsley and petit green peas; steamed red cabbage, onions, and apples.

FIX MEALS—*Get everything ready before cooking*: basmati and veggie rice blend, ginger root and grater, ahi tuna, chopped cilantro, lime juice, toasted sesame oil, organic low-sodium tamari sauce, arugula, and black pepper.

Dinner—Main Course Plan:
7-Color Soups: Clockwise:
purple borscht, zesty
green, red Hungarian,
tan lentil with Canadian
bacon, ginger orange
carrot, and yellow curry.
Center: winter white.

Breakfast—Shakes: Back to my roots. Lower level, left to right: Chocolate banana nut, banana power, strawberry yogurt, Green Meanie, raspberry parfait, Brazilian mocha. Top: purple passion, vanilla peach. Note the 1950s mixer from my dad's soda fountain.

ENJOY DINING—*Menus for Week One*. Day 1: BREAKFAST: strawberry yogurt shake, whole-grain bagel, hummus, fresh orange juice. LUNCH: apricot (peach) melon salad with cottage cheese, wholegrain crackers. DINNER: lime-and-ginger seared ahi tuna, basmati rice medley, and spinach, red pear, avocado, pomegranate salad.

Menus for Week One—Day 2: BREAKFAST: cooked oatmeal, fat-free yogurt, cinnamon sticks, organic raspberry apple-sauce, raisins, low-sodium organic vegetable juice. LUNCH: whole-wheat pita bread stuffed with sunflower sprouts, tomato slices, avocado, lettuce, and grated daikon. DINNER: golden chicken soup; purple radicchio, orange slices, feta cheese, pecans, and dried cranberries; garlic and peppercorn bread, lemon olive oil for dipping, balsamic vinegar dressing.

Rainbow Tomatoes—Red, orange, and yellow carotenoids are the pigments in these tomatoes. Each color has a specific health-promoting property.

Menu plans are meant to be flexible. Families with several members will find that the plan provides just the right amount of food for the week. Smaller families may want to scale back, either by stretching the menu plans beyond seven days or by reducing the amount of ingredients in main course modules. The plans also allow you to enjoy leftovers the next day, a bonus for busy people.

Let's get started by filling in the week-at-a-glance schematic for four weeks. It's followed by day-at-a-glance detailed plans.

WEEK 1

Week One Plans

Week at a Glance

Day	Modules	Recipe	Super Salad	Side Dish(es)
1	Entrée	Lime-and-Ginger–Seared Ahi Tuna	Spinach, pear, avocado, and dried cherries	Basmati Rice Medley
2	Main course	Golden Chicken Soup	Purple radicchio, orange slices, feta cheese, organic pecans	Garlic-and-peppercorn artisan bread
3	Entrée	Red Lentils with Canadian Bacon	Arugula, grapefruit, blueberries, pine nuts	Steamed carrots, broccoli, oregano
4	Main course	Creamy Risotto with Vegetables	Purple leaf lettuce, pears, avocado, cranberries, and sesame seeds	Braised Winter Vegetables
5	Entrée	Pan-Seared Wild Pacific Salmon with Tarragon Aioli	Belgian endive, purple radicchio, mango, pineapple, blueberries, and coconut	Wild and brown rice mix with mushrooms and parsley
6	Free			
7	Entrée	Chicken-and-Turkey Sausage with Sun-Dried Tomatoes, Purple Cabbage, and Red Apples		Steamed brown rice

Day at a Glance

Day 1

BREAKFAST

- Strawberry Yogurt Breakfast Shake (recipe on page 121)
- ½ whole-grain bagel
- 2 tablespoons hummus
- 4 ounces fresh orange juice

LUNCH

- Apricot and melon salad with cottage cheese
- 4 whole-grain crackers

DINNER

- Lime-and-Ginger–Seared Ahi Tuna (recipe on page 121)
- Basmati Rice Medley
- Super Salad: spinach, pear, avocado, and cherries

Day 2

BREAKFAST

- 1 cup cooked organic oatmeal or other unsweetened cereal
- 1 cup fat-free, plain yogurt or soy milk
- ¼ teaspoon cinnamon to sprinkle on cereal
- ½ cup raspberry applesauce
- ¼ cup raisins
- 4 ounces low-sodium, organic vegetable juice

LUNCH

+ Small pita pocket bread with tomatoes, grated daikon, sprouts, lettuce

DINNER

+ Golden Chicken Soup (recipe on page 122)
+ Super Salad: purple radicchio, orange slices, feta cheese, and organic pecans
+ Garlic-and-peppercorn artisan bread

Day 3

BREAKFAST

+ 1 cup strawberries
+ ½ cup yogurt
+ ½ teaspoon grated cinnamon
+ 1 slice whole-wheat toast
+ 2 tablespoons nut butter

LUNCH

+ 2 cups Golden Chicken Soup (from last night's dinner)
+ ½ cup baby carrots

DINNER

+ Red Lentils with Canadian Bacon (recipe on page 123)
+ Super Salad: arugula, grapefruit, blueberries, and pine nuts
+ 1 cup steamed carrots and broccoli with fresh oregano

A New Way of Eating

Day 4

BREAKFAST
- Banana Power Shake (recipe on page 124)
- Whole-grain English muffin with nut butter

LUNCH
- 1 cup Red Lentils with Canadian Bacon (from last night's dinner)
- Small Super Salad with grapefruit and avocado
- Lemon juice or balsamic vinegar to dress the salad

DINNER
- Creamy Risotto with Vegetables (recipe on page 125)
- Braised Winter Vegetables (recipe on page 126)
- Super Salad: purple leaf lettuce, pears, avocado, cranberries, and sesame seeds

Day 5

BREAKFAST
- 1 cup granola
- 1 cup yogurt, fat-free
- ½ cup blackberries
- ½ teaspoon grated cinnamon

LUNCH
- 2 cups baby spinach
- 1 tomato, sliced
- ½ cup tuna, water-packed
- ¼ cup croutons

- 1 tablespoon balsamic vinegar
- ¼ teaspoon black pepper, freshly ground

DINNER
- Pan-Seared Wild Pacific Salmon with Tarragon Aioli (recipe on page 127)
- Super Salad: Belgian endive, purple radicchio, mango, pineapple, blueberries, and unsweetened coconut
- Wild and brown rice mix with mushrooms and parsley (follow package directions; add mushrooms, if desired)

Day 6 or 7: Weekend

BREAKFAST
- Super Scrambled Eggs (recipe on page 129)
- Fruit Cup with Yogurt (recipe on page 129)
- 4 ounces cranberry juice

DINNER
- Chicken-and-Turkey Sausage with Sun-Dried Tomatoes, Purple Cabbage, and Red Apples (recipe on page 130)
- Steamed brown rice (follow package directions)

Shopping Lists

Complete shopping lists are provided in Appendix C. The cold pantry list includes items that need refrigeration, like fresh produce, dairy products, eggs, fish, poultry, and meat. The dry pantry list includes staples you'll need to keep on hand. The wet pantry list includes bottled and canned items, condiments, salsas, and dressings that don't need refrigeration until they're opened. A separate list is included for spices and herbs.

Use the pantry lists from Step Two (pages 57–88) and Appendix C (pages 222–225) to determine which of the following items must be purchased each week.

TAN FOODS

arborio rice	lentils
artisan bread	mixed nuts
basmati rice	nut butter
with dehydrated vegetables	old-fashioned organic oats
brown rice, long-grain	other nonsweetened cereal
buckwheat soba noodles	pita pockets, small
croutons	whole-grain bagel
flaxseed	whole-grain bread
granola	whole-grain crackers
hummus	wild and brown rice mix

CREAMY WHITE FOODS

ahi tuna, fresh	salmon, wild Pacific
Canadian bacon	strawberry whey protein
chicken	powder
chicken-and-turkey sausage	tuna (water-packed)
with sun-dried tomatoes	yogurt (plain, fat-free)

RAINBOW-COLORED FOODS

apples, red	limes
applesauce, raspberry	mushrooms
avocados	onions
blackberries	orange juice
blueberries	papaya
carrots, baby	pears
cranberry juice	pineapple

garlic
ginger root, fresh
grapes, green
greens, baby mixed
greens, braising
leeks
lemons

raisins
baby spinach leaves
strawberries
fresh tarragon
tomatoes
organic vegetable juice
(low-salt)

Condiments

arrowroot powder
balsamic vinegar
Chinese five-spice powder
cinnamon
curry powder
four-color pepper
green chili sauce

nutmeg
organic extra virgin olive oil
peanut oil
seasoned salt
sesame oil
tamari sauce, low-sodium
white wine, dry

Steamed Brown Rice

SEASON	All
PREPARATION TIME	45 minutes
SERVINGS	4 (1 cup each)

NUTRITION FACTS
calories	219
total fat	1.8 grams
saturated fat	0.4 grams
cholesterol	0 milligrams
sodium	355 milligrams
carbohydrate	45.3 grams
fiber	3.5 grams
protein	5.5 gram.

INGREDIENTS

1 cup long-grain brown rice

1¾ cups water

½ teaspoon soup base, fat-free

¼ cup parsley, chopped (optional)

DIRECTIONS

1. Wash rice and place in steamer insert.

2. Add water, soup base, and chopped parsley.

3. Cover and set steamer for 45 minutes.

4. When steaming is complete, allow rice to set 5 minutes, then fluff with a fork.

A NEW WAY OF EATING

Strawberry Yogurt Breakfast Shake

NUTRITION FACTS
calories 304
total fat 1.3 grams
saturated fat 0.4 gram
cholesterol 4.5 milligrams
sodium 72 milligrams
carbohydrate 44.9 grams
fiber 4.5 grams
protein 28.9 grams

INGREDIENTS

½ cup strawberries, fresh or frozen

½ cup banana, cut into chunks

¼ cup orange juice, fresh

⅛ cup plain, fat-free yogurt

½ cup strawberry whey protein isolate powder (31 grams)

DIRECTIONS

Mix all items in a blender until smooth.

Lime-and-Ginger–Seared Ahi Tuna

SEASON
All

PREPARATION TIME
20 minutes

SERVINGS
2 (4 ounces each)

NUTRITION FACTS
calories 213
total fat 8.3 grams
saturated fat 1.3 grams
cholesterol 52 milligrams
sodium 590 milligrams
carbohydrate 5.7 grams
fiber 1.4 grams
protein 29.1 grams

NOTE: *Super Salad: spinach, pear, avocado, and dried cherries with sesame seeds and creamy sesame seed dressing*

INGREDIENTS

1 tablespoon ginger root, peeled and grated

2 tablespoon lime juice

1 teaspoon sesame oil

¼ teaspoon black pepper

⅛ cup soy sauce, low-sodium

8 ounces ahi tuna

4 ounces arugula

1 tablespoon cilantro leaves, chopped

DIRECTIONS

1. Slice and grate ginger root.

2. Combine ginger, lime juice, pepper, sesame oil, and soy sauce.

3. Marinate tuna for at least 1 hour (preferably overnight). Reserve marinade in refrigerator.

4. Wash and cut arugula into bite-sized pieces; arrange on two plates. Ahi can also be pan seared for same time.

5. Prepare hot coals and grill ahi approximately 4 minutes on each side.

6. Place grilled tuna over arugula; drizzle with reserved marinade.

7. Sprinkle cilantro over each piece of tuna.

Step Three: Fix Your Meals

Golden Chicken Soup

SEASON
Cool

PREPARATION TIME
25 minutes

SERVINGS
4 (2 cups each)

NUTRITION FACTS
calories 210
total fat 1.1 grams
saturated fat 0.3 grams
cholesterol 39 milligrams
sodium 689 milligrams
carbohydrate 31.8 grams
fiber 3.5 grams
protein 18.7 grams

NOTE: *Super Salad: purple radicchio, orange slices, feta cheese, and organic pecans with creamy Caesar dressing*

INGREDIENTS

8 ounces chicken breast, boneless and skinless

1 pound butternut squash, peeled, seeded, and diced into 1-inch squares

2 cups leeks (bulb and lower leaves), diced

⅓ cup parsley, minced

1 cup celery, medium dice

1 tablespoon soup base (fat-free)

1 quart water

2 tablespoons arrowroot

¾ teaspoon black pepper

1 cup sour cream, fat-free

¼ cup chives, chopped

DIRECTIONS

1. Steam or bake chicken breast without adding any oil. Cut into bite-sized chunks and set aside.

2. Add butternut squash, leeks, parsley, and celery to a 3½-quart pressure cooker.

3. Add soup base, water, and black pepper. Process at 8 psi 15 minutes. Or, cook on top of stove in a covered pot for 1 hour.

4. Allow pressure to drop of its own accord.

5. Allow soup to cool until it can be easily handled, then purée it in a blender.

6. Dissolve arrowroot in sour cream and place in blender with the last batch of soup.

7. Return processed soup and sour cream mixture to pot and heat to serving temperature.

8. Ladle soup into bowls and sprinkle chives over each serving.

Red Lentils with Canadian Bacon

SEASON
All

PREPARATION TIME
20 minutes

SERVINGS
6 (1 cup each)

NUTRITION FACTS

calories	305
total fat	2.4 grams
saturated fat	0.6 grams
cholesterol	11 milligrams
sodium	595 milligrams
carbohydrate	46.8 grams
fiber	22.1 grams
protein	24 grams

SUPER SALAD: *arugula, grapefruit, blueberries, and pine nuts with organic walnut oil and lemon juice*

INGREDIENTS

4 ounces Canadian bacon

1 cups carrots, peeled and sliced ¼ inch thick

1 cup red onions, chopped

1 cup celery, diced

½ cup green bell peppers, diced

½ cup red bell peppers, diced

1 large yellow bell pepper, diced

2 cups red lentils

½ cup cilantro, minced

4 cups water

1 teaspoon seasoned salt

DIRECTIONS

1. Cut bacon into bite-sized pieces and brown lightly in 3½-quart pressure cooker.

2. Add onions, celery, and bell peppers to bacon and sauté over medium heat until onions are translucent.

3. Wash lentils, discarding any that are broken, and add them to vegetables.

4. Add cilantro, water, and salt.

5. Cover the pressure cooker and bring pressure to the second red ring (15 psi). Cook 15 minutes and let pressure drop of its own accord. Or, cook on top of stove in a covered pot for 1 hour.

6. Serve as a main dish with vegetables and a salad.

Banana Power Shake

SEASON
All

PREPARATION TIME
10 minutes

SERVINGS
1 (12 ounces)

NUTRITION FACTS

calories	295
total fat	2 grams
saturated fat	0.5 grams
cholesterol	6.31 milligrams
sodium	118 milligrams
carbohydrate	37.8 grams
fiber	2.5 grams
protein	31.8 grams

INGREDIENTS

6 tablespoons pineapple juice, bottled and unsweetened

¼ cup banana, sliced

1 teaspoon flaxseed

½ cup vanilla whey protein isolate powder (31 grams)

6 tablespoons plain, nonfat yogurt

pinch of stevia or 1 teaspoon erythritol to sweeten

DIRECTIONS

1. Mix ingredients together in a blender or drink mixer.

2. Add ice if desired.

Creamy Risotto with Vegetables

SEASON
All

PREPARATION TIME
30 minutes

SERVINGS
8 (1 cup each)

NUTRITION FACTS

calories	257
total fat	5.7 grams
saturated fat	1.8 grams
cholesterol	5 milligrams
sodium	313 milligrams
carbohydrate	44.6 grams
fiber	2.7 grams
protein	7.1 grams

INGREDIENTS

- **4 cups water**
- **2 teaspoons soup base, fat-free**
- **2 tablespoons extra virgin olive oil pressed with Meyer lemon***
- **⅓ cup onions, chopped**
- **¼ cup celery, chopped**
- **¼ cup carrots, chopped**
- **¼ cup yellow bell pepper, chopped**
- **¼ cup red bell pepper, chopped**
- **1 clove garlic, minced or pressed**
- **2 cups arborio rice**
- **1 cup dry, white wine**
- **¼ teaspoon salt**
- **½ teaspoon pepper, freshly ground**
- **½ cup Parmesan cheese, grated**
- **1 cup petite green peas, no added salt**

* See Appendix D.

DIRECTIONS

1. In a medium saucepan, add soup base to water and bring to a boil.

2. In a large pot, heat olive oil over moderately low heat. Add onion, celery, carrots, peppers, and garlic.

3. Cook until onion is translucent.

4. Add rice to pot and stir until it begins to turn opaque, approximately 2 minutes.

5. Add wine and salt and stir frequently until all wine has been absorbed.

6. Add ½ cup of the simmering broth and stir frequently until broth has been completely absorbed. The rice and broth should bubble gently; adjust heat as needed.

7. Continue adding broth in ½-cup increments until rice is tender, 25 to 30 minutes in all. Add additional broth if needed to keep rice moist.

8. Add peas and mix thoroughly to warm through.

9. Stir in pepper and Parmesan and serve.

Braised Winter Vegetables

SEASON
Cool

PREPARATION TIME
20 minutes

SERVINGS
6 (2 cups each)

NUTRITION FACTS
calories	150
total fat	7.2 grams
saturated fat	1 gram
cholesterol	0 milligrams
sodium	361 milligrams
carbohydrate	16.2 grams
fiber	3.5 grams
protein	4.7 grams

SUPER SALAD: *purple leaf lettuce, sliced pears, avocado, dried cranberries, and sesame seeds with creamy sesame dressing*

INGREDIENTS

- **8 cups Swiss chard leaves or mixed braising greens**
- **2 cups butternut squash, peeled, seeded, and chopped into bite-sized pieces**
- **2 tablespoons fresh garlic, minced or pressed**
- **½ cup well cleaned leek (bulb and lower leaves), sliced crosswise into small rings**
- **1 tablespoon ginger root, grated**
- **1 tablespoon toasted sesame oil**
- **1½ tablespoon tamari sauce, low-sodium**
- **2 teaspoons rice vinegar**
- **2 teaspoons arrowroot**
- **1 teaspoon Chinese five-spice powder**
- **1 tablespoon peanut oil**
- **2 tablespoons sesame seeds**
- **8 ounces buckwheat soba noodles, prepared according to package directions**

DIRECTIONS

1. Cut most stems from Swiss chard. (If braising greens are used, these are usually young tender leaves that don't need trimming.) Wash and dry leaves, chop into bite-sized pieces, set aside.

2. Mix oil, tamari sauce, rice vinegar, arrowroot, and Chinese five-spice powder and set aside.

3. Heat peanut oil in the bottom of a large wok.

4. Add butternut squash, garlic, leek, and ginger.

5. Stir vegetables over high heat, turning frequently until squash begins to soften, approximately 6 minutes.

6. Add chard or braising greens and continue to stir until greens are wilted and squash is tender, approximately 10 minutes.

7. Stir in sauce (oil, tamari, rice vinegar, arrowroot, and five spice) and heat through until slightly thickened.

8. Add sesame seeds and serve with buckwheat soba noodles.

Pan-Seared Wild Pacific Salmon with Tarragon Aioli

SEASON
All, especially when wild
salmon available

PREPARATION TIME
25 minutes

SERVINGS
2 (6 ounces each)

NUTRITION FACTS
calories 238
total fat 91 grams
saturated fat 10 grams
cholesterol 76 milligrams
sodium 78 milligrams
carbohydrate 2 grams
fiber 1 gram
protein 37 grams

Salmon

INGREDIENTS

**12 ounces wild Pacific
salmon fillets**

**1 cup young arugula
leaves**

1 lemon, cut in wedges

DIRECTIONS

1. Wash and pat salmon fillets
   dry.

2. Using as little oil as possible,
   rub it on a nonstick pan to
   coat. Remove any excess.

3. Heat pan just until it barely
   begins to smoke. Watch carefully, because smoking means
   the oil is breaking down and
   will not taste the same.

4. Place salmon flesh-side down
   in pan and brown 5 minutes.

5. Turn salmon over onto skin-
   side and brown an additional
   5 to 7 minutes, depending on
   thickness of fillets. Salmon
   should be cooked through, but
   still firm. Do not overcook!

6. Immediately place on a bed of
   arugula and top with 1 tablespoon of tarragon aioli. Serve
   lemon wedges on side.

(R E C I P E   C O N T I N U E S)

Step Three: Fix Your Meals

NUTRITION FACTS

calories	101
total fat	11 grams
saturated fat	1.6 grams
cholesterol	11 milligrams
sodium	23 milligrams
carbohydrate	0.2 grams
fiber	0 grams
protein	0.3 grams

SUPER SALAD: *Belgian endive, purple radicchio, mango, pineapple, blueberries, and shredded coconut with raspberry vinaigrette*

Tarragon Aioli

INGREDIENTS

¼ cup fresh tarragon leaves

1 egg, beaten

2 tablespoons lemon juice

¼ teaspoon seasoned salt

¼ teaspoon yellow mustard seed, powdered

1 cup organic extra virgin olive oil

DIRECTIONS

1. Choose 4 large sprigs of tarragon. Wash carefully and pat dry. Remove leaves and chop coarsely. Set aside.

2. Place egg, lemon juice, salt, and powdered mustard seed into blender and cover.

3. Turn blender to speed 4 or "beat" speed.

4. After 5 seconds, remove center section from cover of blender and slowly pour oil into the container while blades are rotating.

5. Stop motor and use a spatula, if needed, to blend the last of the oil into the mixture. All oil should be completely blended into a creamy mixture.

6. Add chopped tarragon and blend in just until tarragon is completely mixed in.

SUGGESTION: *Use leftover aioli on broccoli or other steamed vebetables, on poached eggs, chicken or fish.*

Super Scrambled Eggs

NUTRITION FACTS
calories	143
total fat	10.6 grams
saturated fat	2.6 grams
cholesterol	258 milligrams
sodium	156 milligrams
carbohydrate	3.1 grams
fiber	1.1 grams
protein	8.7 grams

INGREDIENTS

2 eggs, scrambled

SERVE ON

1 cup baby greens topped with

1 tablespoon chili sauce

Fruit Cup with Yogurt

NUTRITION FACTS
calories	148
total fat	1.2 grams
saturated fat	0.5 grams
cholesterol	1 milligram
sodium	51 milligrams
carbohydrate	29.6 grams
fiber	31 grams
protein	4.4 grams

INGREDIENTS

1 cup pineapple, cut into chunks

¼ cup blueberries

¼ cup fat-free, plain yogurt on top of fruit

¼ teaspoon nutmeg to flavor fruit and yogurt

Chicken-and-Turkey Sausage with Sun-Dried Tomatoes, Purple Cabbage, and Red Apples

SEASON
All

PREPARATION TIME
45 minutes

SERVINGS
2 (1 sausage link and
2 cups vegetables each
serving)

NUTRITION FACTS

calories	240
total fat	7.6 grams
saturated fat	2 grams
cholesterol	55 milligrams
sodium	601 milligrams
carbohydrate	24.9 grams
fiber	5.5 grams
protein	17.9 grams

NOTE: *These sausages, which generally come four to a package, are precooked. You can double this recipe to enjoy the leftover sausages, cabbage, and apples in pita bread for lunch the next day.*

INGREDIENTS

4 cups purple cabbage, shredded

2 cups red apples with skin, sliced

1 cup onions, sliced

⅓ cup cranberry juice

1 teaspoon of fennel or caraway seeds

½ teaspoon black pepper, freshly ground

4 chicken-and-turkey sausages with sun-dried tomatoes

DIRECTIONS

1. Layer cabbage, apples, and onions in a large skillet or wok.

2. Add cranberry juice, fennel or caraway seeds, and black pepper.

3. Add sausages and cover and steam until vegetables are soft.

4. Serve with steamed brown rice.

WEEK 2

Week Two Plans

Week at a Glance

Day	Modules	Recipe	Super Salad	Side Dish(es)
1	Entrée	Tequila Sole with Avocado Lime Cream	Wilted Spinach and Orange	Golden Couscous with Parsley and Green Peas
2	Main course	Split-Pea Soup with Ham	Apple and Arugula Salad	Whole-grain rye bread
3	Entrée	Mediterranean Meat Loaf	Purple radicchio, yellow pear, and avocado with poppy seeds	Garlic Mashed Potatoes
4	Main course	Savory Beef Stew	Mesclun, raspberries, kiwi, and avocados	Whole-grain biscuits
5	Entrée	Pecan-Crusted Chicken with Mustard Dipping Sauce	Belgian endive, kiwi, and orange slices	Blanched Edamame with Slivered Almonds
6	Free			
7	Entrée	Grilled Rib-Eye Steak with Cherry Salsa	Romaine lettuce, mini mixed bell peppers, cherry tomatoes, and cucumbers	Summer Vegetable Grill

Day 1

BREAKFAST

+ 1 cup granola with ½ cup yogurt
+ ½ cup strawberries

- 4 ounces fresh tangerine juice

LUNCH
- Pita pocket with leftover chicken-and-turkey sausage sliced lengthwise, purple cabbage and red apples (or substitute steamed brown rice for the pita pocket)

DINNER
- Tequila Sole with Avocado Lime Cream (recipe on page 138)
- Golden Couscous with Parsley and Green Peas (recipe on page 139)
- Super Salad: Wilted Spinach and Orange (recipe on page 140)

Day 2

BREAKFAST
- Banana Chocolate Nut Shake (recipe on page 141)
- ½ whole-grain English muffin
- 2 tablespoons sesame butter

LUNCH
Pita pocket with:
- ½ cup mixed bean sprouts
- ½ cup tomato slices
- ¼ cup cucumber

DINNER
- Split-Pea Soup with Ham (recipe on page 141)
- Whole-grain rye bread

+ Super Salad: apple and arugula

Day 3

BREAKFAST
+ 1 cup granola with almonds
+ ½ cup yogurt, plain, low-fat
+ cinnamon
+ 4 ounces tomato juice

LUNCH
+ Split-Pea Soup with Ham left over from dinner

DINNER
+ Mediterranean Meat Loaf (recipe on page 143)
+ Garlic Mashed Potatoes (recipe on page 144)
+ Super Salad: purple radicchio, yellow pear, and avocado with poppy seeds

Day 4

BREAKFAST
+ Strawberry Yogurt Breakfast Shake (recipe on page 121)
+ 1 slice whole-grain toast with 1 tablespoon nut butter

LUNCH
+ Super Salad: cottage cheese and tropical fruit with raspberry vinaigrette

DINNER
+ Savory Beef Stew (recipe on page 145)

- 2 whole-grain biscuits
- Super Salad: mesclun, raspberries, kiwi, and avocados

Day 5

BREAKFAST
- 1 cup granola with ½ cup almond milk
- ½ cup blueberries
- 4 ounces low-salt, organic vegetable juice

LUNCH
- 2 cups Savory Beef Stew from dinner

DINNER
- Pecan-Crusted Chicken with Mustard Dipping Sauce (recipe on page 146)
- Blanched Edamame with Slivered Almonds (recipe on page 148)
- Super Salad: Belgian endive, kiwi, and orange slices

Day 6 or 7: Weekend

BREAKFAST
- Blueberry Oat Muffin (recipe on page 149)
- 2 scrambled eggs with ½ cup mixed bell peppers and ¼ cup chopped arugula
- Fruit Cup with Yogurt (recipe on page 129)

DINNER
- Grilled Rib-Eye Steak with Cherry Salsa (recipe on page 150)

- Summer Vegetable Grill (recipe on page 151)
- Super Salad: romaine lettuce, mini mixed bell peppers, cherry tomatoes, and cucumbers

Shopping List

Tan Foods

barley, organic	split peas
couscous, organic	walnuts, organic
granola, organic	whole-grain bagels
pecans, organic	whole-grain bread
pita pockets, small	whole-grain English muffins
sesame butter	

White Foods

almond milk	ham (99% fat-free)
beef round, lean	milk, organic
bleu cheese	rib-eye steak, lean
chicken breast	sole, filet of
chocolate whey powder	turkey, ground
cottage cheese, low-fat	yogurt
cream cheese, low-fat	

Rainbow-Colored Foods

arugula	blueberries
avocado	carrots
bananas	celery
bell peppers (red, yellow, and orange)	cherries
	cucumbers

fire-roasted tomatoes, Muir-
Glen canned

garlic

green edamame pods

jalapeño pepper

Japanese eggplant

limes or lime juice

low-salt, organic vegetable juice

mixed bean sprouts

oranges

peas, petite frozen

purple cabbage

purple onions

raspberries

red apples

red grapes

red-skinned potatoes

russet potatoes

salsa

scallions

spinach, organic baby

strawberries

sun-dried tomatoes

tarragon, fresh

tomatoes

Vidalia onions

watermelon

yellow crook-necked squash

zucchini

MISCELLANEOUS
tequila

Tequila Sole with Avocado Lime Cream

Sole

SEASON
Summer

PREPARATION TIME
30 minutes

SERVINGS
2 people

NUTRITION FACTS

calories	127
total fat	1.5 grams
saturated fat	0.3 grams
cholesterol	56 milligrams
sodium	289 milligrams
carbohydrate	6 grams
fiber	1.1 grams
protein	22.2 grams

INGREDIENTS

8 ounces sole (or flounder)

1 tablespoon lime juice

1 ounce tequila

¼ teaspoon seasoned salt

½ cup zucchini, roasted and diced into 1-inch pieces

½ cup red bell pepper, roasted and diced into 1-inch pieces

½ cup yellow bell pepper, roasted and diced into 1-inch pieces

DIRECTIONS

1. Wash sole and pat dry.

2. Marinate 15 minutes in lime juice, tequila, and salt. While sole is marinating, prepare lime cream.

3. Roll each filet into a round spiral, skin inside, and steam 10 minutes.

4. Arrange over a bed of roasted zucchini and bell peppers.

5. Drizzle Avocado Lime Cream (see recipe below) on top.

6. Serve with a Super Salad of wilted spinach, oranges, onions, and pecans and a side dish of organic couscous.

Avocado Lime Cream

PREPARATION TIME
20 minutes

SERVINGS
8 (1 tablespoon)

NUTRITION FACTS
calories 115
total fat 10.3 grams
saturated fat 3.8 grams
cholesterol 16 milligrams
sodium 63 milligrams
carbohydrate 3.4 grams
fiber 1.5 grams
protein 2.1 grams

INGREDIENTS

¾ cup avocado, diced *¼ c*

⅛ cup chicken broth,
low-sodium *tsp*

4 ounces cream cheese *1 oz*

juice of ½ lime

1 cup cilantro, chopped *¼ c*

¾ cup spring onions or
scallions, chopped *¼ c*

1 tablespoon hot red salsa,
bottled

1 tablespoon garlic,
minced *1 clove*

1 tablespoon almond or
vegetable oil *¼ tbsp*

DIRECTIONS

1. Add all ingredients to a food
   processor and purée.

2. Use as drizzle.

3. Garnish with cilantro sprigs,
   cherry tomatoes, or black
   olives.

Golden Couscous with Parsley and Green Peas

SEASON
All

PREPARATION TIME
10 minutes

SERVINGS
4 (½ cup each)

NUTRITION FACTS
calories 206
total fat 2.4 grams
saturated fat 0.2 grams
cholesterol 0 milligrams
sodium 28 milligrams
carbohydrate 39.1 grams
fiber 3.2 grams
protein 7.1 grams

INGREDIENTS

1¼ cup water

2 teaspoons macadamia
nut oil or butter

1 cup golden organic
couscous

¼ cup parsley, chopped

½ cup frozen petite peas,
salt-free

DIRECTIONS

1. Bring water to a boil. Add oil
   or butter.

2. Stir in couscous, parsley, and
   peas.

3. Remove from heat and let
   stand 5 minutes.

4. Fluff with a fork and serve.

Wilted Spinach and Orange Salad

SEASON
All

PREPARATION TIME
15 minutes

SERVINGS
2

NUTRITION FACTS

calories	268
total fat	10.5 grams
saturated fat	1.2 grams
cholesterol	0 milligrams
sodium	100 milligrams
carbohydrate	36.4 grams
fiber	12 grams
protein	6.8 grams

INGREDIENTS

- zest from 1 orange
- 2 cups orange slices (approximately 2 oranges)
- 8 cups organic baby spinach
- ¼ cup Vidalia onions
- ¼ cup red wine vinegar
- 2 teaspoons organic extra virgin olive oil
- 2 tablespoons fresh tarragon leaves, minced
- 2 tablespoons organic pecans (broken pieces)

DIRECTIONS

1. Grate or zest peel from one orange before slicing; set zest aside.

2. Peel oranges and slice them thinly and horizontally, reserving juice that collects during slicing.

3. Wash and dry baby spinach. If using larger spinach, break up large leaves and discard woody stems.

4. Slice onions into whole rings.

5. To prepare the dressing, mix vinegar, olive oil, tarragon, orange zest, and leftover orange juice in a bowl. Whisk together and set aside.

6. Place spinach and onion rings in a large wok with a nonstick surface. Add ¼ cup water, cover, and steam just until spinach wilts, but remains bright green.

7. Arrange on two salad plates, top with orange slices, and sprinkle pecans over top.

8. Sprinkle ⅛ cup dressing over each salad.

Banana Chocolate Nut Shake

NUTRITION FACTS

calories	372
total fat	6.5 grams
saturated fat	2.3 grams
cholesterol	4.5 milligrams
sodium	170 milligrams
carbohydrate	42.8 grams
fiber	3.3 grams
protein	35.4 grams

INGREDIENTS

- 1 cup almond nut milk
- ½ cup chocolate whey protein isolate powder (31 grams)
- ½ cup banana, sliced
- 1 tablespoon almonds, chopped

DIRECTIONS

Mix all ingredients in a blender.

Split-Pea Soup with Ham

SEASON
All

PREPARATION TIME
20 minutes

SERVINGS
10 (1½ cups each)

NUTRITION FACTS

calories	257
total fat	4.1 grams
saturated fat	0.9 grams
cholesterol	16 milligrams
sodium	607 milligrams
carbohydrate	37.2 grams
fiber	13.1 grams
protein	18 grams

INGREDIENTS

- 2 tablespoons organic extra virgin olive oil
- 1 cup onions, diced
- 2 cloves garlic, minced or pressed
- 2 cups carrots, diced
- 2 cups split peas, washed (remove broken peas)
- 1 teaspoon cumin, powdered
- 1 teaspoon black pepper, freshly ground
- ½ cup barley
- 2 quarts water
- 2 teaspoons soup base, fat-free
- 1 cup celery, diced
- ½ cup cilantro, chopped
- 12 ounces fully cooked ham (99% fat-free), diced

DIRECTIONS

1. Heat olive oil in a 5-quart kettle.
2. Lightly sauté onions and garlic.
3. Add carrots, split peas, cumin, black pepper, barley, water, and soup base.
4. Cover pot and simmer for 1 hour.
5. Just before end of cooking, add celery and cilantro.
6. Turn off heat and add ham.
7. Serve with Apple and Arugula Salad and whole-grain rye bread.

Apple and Arugula Salad

SEASON
All

SERVINGS
2

NUTRITION FACTS

calories	397
total fat	26.6 grams
saturated fat	9.9 grams
cholesterol	32 milligrams
sodium	624 milligrams
carbohydrate	26.2 grams
fiber	5.3 grams
protein	12.3 grams

INGREDIENTS

4 cups arugula, torn into bite-sized pieces

2 cups red apples, sliced with skin on

¼ cup shredded daikon or jicama

3 tablespoons lemon juice

⅛ cup crumbled bleu cheese

2 tablespoons organic walnut oil

DIRECTIONS

1. Place arugula on two salad plates.

2. Top with apples and daikon or jicama; sprinkle with lemon juice.

3. Sprinkle plates with bleu cheese.

4. Drizzle walnut oil over both salads.

Mediterranean Meat Loaf

SEASON
All

PREPARATION TIME
20 minutes

SERVINGS
6 (1-inch slice each)

NUTRITION FACTS

calories	271
total fat	12.1 grams
saturated fat	3.7 grams
cholesterol	97 milligrams
sodium	370 milligrams
carbohydrate	15.1 grams
fiber	3.3 grams
protein	25.6 grams

INGREDIENTS

- ¼ cup sun-dried tomatoes
- 1 pound baby spinach, raw
- ½ cup onions, diced
- ¼ cup feta cheese, crumbled
- 1½ pounds ground turkey
- 1 cup regular organic oats (not instant)
- 1 teaspoon garlic powder
- 1 teaspoon oregano, ground
- ¼ teaspoon seasoned salt
- ¼ teaspoon black pepper
- ½ cup milk, low-fat

DIRECTIONS

1. Heat oven to 400°F.

2. Soften tomatoes according to package directions.

3. In a skillet coated with cooking spray, cook spinach and onion just until wilted. Stir in feta cheese and set mixture aside.

4. In a large bowl combine turkey, oats, garlic powder, oregano, salt, black pepper, milk, and sun-dried tomatoes. Mix thoroughly.

5. Shape two-thirds of the turkey mixture into a 9×6-inch loaf and place in a 13×9-inch baking dish. Make an indentation along the center of the turkey mixture, leaving approximately 1½ inches around the edges of the loaf. Fill with spinach mixture and cover with the remaining turkey mixture to completely cover spinach filling. Pinch the edges to seal.

6. Bake 30 to 35 minutes or until juices run clear when loaf is pierced with a fork. Let stand 5 minutes before slicing.

Garlic Mashed Potatoes

SEASON
All

PREPARATION TIME
30 minutes

SERVINGS
6 (1 cup each)

NUTRITION FACTS

calories	106
total fat	2.5 grams
saturated fat	1.5 grams
cholesterol	7 milligrams
sodium	206 milligrams
carbohydrate	17.9 grams
fiber	1.5 grams
protein	3 grams

INGREDIENTS

1 pound russet potatoes, peeled or with skins, scrubbed, for additional fiber

1 cup water

2 to 3 cloves garlic (3 large cloves = approximately 1½ teaspoons), minced or pressed

1 cup milk, low-fat (for added flavor use 1 cup fat-free sour cream)

1 tablespoon butter, unsalted

1 teaspoon seasoned salt

¼ teaspoon black pepper, freshly ground

DIRECTIONS

1. Cut potatoes into large chunks and add water.

2. Cover and cook until potatoes are tender, approximately 20 minutes.

3. Meanwhile, add garlic to milk and heat over low heat just to the boiling point. If using sour cream, heat just until warm.

4. Add butter.

5. When cooked potatoes are soft, mash them in a mixer using the whipping attachment.

6. When potatoes are mashed, slowly add milk (or sour cream), garlic, and butter mixture while mixer is running, until whipped. Season with salt and pepper.

Savory Beef Stew

SEASON
Winter

PREPARATION TIME
30 minutes

SERVINGS
6 (2 cups each)

NUTRITION FACTS

calories	245
fat	47 grams total
saturated fat	5.2 grams
cholesterol	45 milligrams
sodium	618 milligrams
carbohydrate	28.8 grams
fiber	4.7 grams
protein	20.7 grams

SUPER SALAD: *mesclun, rasp-berries, kiwi, and avocados*

INGREDIENTS

- **1 pound lean beef round, cut into 1-inch pieces**
- **1½ cups mushrooms, large dice**
- **1 cup onion, large dice**
- **2 cups carrots, large dice**
- **1 cup celery, large dice**
- **1 pound small red-skinned potatoes, whole**
- **2 cups fire-roasted tomatoes, large dice**
- **2 cups water**
- **1 tablespoon soup base, fat-free**
- **1 tablespoon bay leaf, crumbled**
- **1 tablespoon oregano, ground**
- **1 teaspoon black pepper**
- **¼ cup curly leaf parsley, minced**

DIRECTIONS

1. Brown beef in a 3½-quart pressure cooker that has been coated with cooking spray.
2. Add mushrooms, onion, carrots, celery, potatoes, and tomatoes.
3. Add water, soup base, bay leaf, oregano, and black pepper.
4. Lock lid in place and bring pressure to second red ring (15 psi).
5. Cook 15 minutes.
6. Allow pressure to drop of its own accord.
7. Serve stew in shallow bowls and top with minced parsley.

Pecan-Crusted Chicken with Mustard Dipping Sauce

Chicken

SEASON
Winter

PREPARATION TIME
20 minutes

SERVINGS
2 (4 ounces chicken each)

NUTRITION FACTS

calories	426
total fat	25.1 grams
saturated fat	3.2 grams
cholesterol	155 milligrams
sodium	400 milligrams
carbohydrate	14.6 grams
fiber	3 grams
protein	35.2 grams

INGREDIENTS

½ cup organic pecans

2 teaspoons arrowroot

1 teaspoon thyme, ground

1 teaspoon paprika

¼ teaspoon salt

⅛ teaspoon cayenne

1 egg

2 tablespoon water

8 ounces boneless chicken breast, skinned and cut into two pieces

DIRECTIONS

1. In food processor, pulse pecans with arrowroot, thyme, paprika, salt, and cayenne until nuts are finely chopped.

2. Whisk egg and water in a small bowl. Dip each chicken piece in the egg and water mixture, then in the nut mixture.

3. Coat a large frying pan with cooking spray and place over low heat. Place the chicken in the pan and cook for 5 minutes. Turn and continue cooking until chicken is golden brown, 5 to 6 minutes longer. Arrange coated chicken pieces on a rack in a broiler or baking pan. Bake at 375°F 40 minutes.

NUTRITION FACTS

Calories	426
total fat	25.1 grams
saturated fat	3.2 grams
cholesterol	155 milligrams
sodium	400 milligrams
carbohydrate	14.6 grams
fiber	3 grams
protein	35.2 grams

Mustard Dipping Sauce

INGREDIENTS

½ cup yogurt, plain, fat-free

2 tablespoons Dijon mustard

½ teaspoon white-wine vinegar

¼ teaspoon honey

2 tablespoons parsley

pinch of cayenne

DIRECTIONS

While chicken breasts bake, combine yogurt, mustard, vinegar, honey, parsley, and cayenne in a small bowl. Serve chicken with mustard dipping sauce. For variation, mix curry powder with mustard sauce.

Blanched Edamame with Slivered Almonds

Eat edamame with your hands by pulling the pods between your front teeth to remove the savory beans inside. The pods will have absorbed the salt water and add a savory zest as you extract the beans. If this method doesn't appeal to you, you can open the pods by hand and squeeze the beans out. Perhaps this is best reserved for those in need of extra time to chill out! Any way you have it, edamame are a great snack as well as a wonderful addition to any meal.

INGREDIENTS

- **4 cups fresh edamame pods (green soybeans)**
- **6 cups water**
- **1 teaspoon salt**
- **1 tablespoon organic olive oil**
- **¼ cup slivered almonds**

DIRECTIONS

1. Bring water to a boil in a 3- or 4-quart saucepan.

2. Add salt and edamame and cook until tender-crisp, approximately 1½ to 2 minutes.

3. Drain edamame, shock in ice water, drain again and pat dry.

4. Toss edamame with oil and slivered almonds.

Blueberry Oat Muffins

SEASON
Any

PREPARATION TIME
35 minutes

SERVINGS
12 muffins (1 per serving)

NUTRITION FACTS

calories	151
total fat	6.2 grams
saturated fat	0.9 grams
cholesterol	18 milligrams
sodium	178 milligrams
carbohydrate	19.2 grams
fiber	3.2 grams
protein	4.6 grams

INGREDIENTS

- 1 cup quick-cooking rolled organic oats
- ¾ cup buttermilk or fat-free yogurt
- 1 cup organic oat or other whole-grain flour
- 1 teaspoon aluminum-free baking powder (available in natural foods markets and some grocery stores)
- ½ teaspoon baking soda
- ½ teaspoon salt
- 1 egg, beaten
- ¼ cup erythritol* or Sucanat
- 2 teaspoons cinnamon, ground
- ½ teaspoon nutmeg, ground
- ¼ cup macadamia nut or organic walnut oil
- 1⅓ cup fresh blueberries, washed and dried

DIRECTIONS

1. Measure oats and buttermilk into a bowl and allow to stand while you prepare muffin cups and remaining ingredients.

2. Lightly spray muffin-cup tray with cooking spray and set aside.

3. In a mixing bowl sift together flour, baking powder, soda, and salt.

4. In a separate bowl mix egg, erythritol, cinnamon, nutmeg, and oil.

5. Add egg mixture to oats and buttermilk, alternating with flour mixture. Combine just until ingredients are blended. *Do not over-mix.*

6. Gently fold in blueberries.

7. Fill muffin cups two-thirds full.

8. Bake at 400°F 20 minutes.

*See Appendix D.

Grilled Rib-Eye Steak with Cherry Salsa

SEASON
All

PREPARATION TIME
20 minutes,
plus time to marinate

SERVINGS
2 (6 ounces each)

NUTRITION FACTS
calories   370
total fat   19.9 grams
saturated fat   8 grams
cholesterol   136 milligrams
sodium   117 milligrams
carbohydrate   0 grams
fiber   0 grams
protein   47.7 grams

NUTRITION FACTS
calories   21
total fat   0.2 grams
saturated fat   0 grams
cholesterol   0 milligrams
sodium   66 milligrams
carbohydrate   4.4 grams
fiber   0 grams
protein   0.3 grams

NOTE: *This recipe, a great complement to other grilled meats, fish, and poultry, comes to us courtesy of my friend, Joan Jackson. Joan is a well-known food consultant andprior to her move to Victoria, British Columbia, the food editor for Chico's Enterprise Record.*

Steak

INGREDIENTS

12 ounces beef rib-eye steak (chicken or pork also work well in this recipe)

Cherry Salsa (see recipe below)

DIRECTIONS

1. Marinate in ⅔ of the Cherry Salsa for at least 1 hour (preferably overnight).

2. Prepare charcoal, and when it's hot, grill the steak.

3. Serve with remaining Cherry Salsa on the side.

Cherry Salsa

INGREDIENTS

1 cup cherries, pitted and halved

2 tablespoons red bell pepper, fine dice

1 tablespoon onion, fine dice

1 jalapeño pepper

1 tablespoon lime juice

2 tablespoons basil, minced

¼ teaspoon seasoned salt

DIRECTIONS

1. Cut jalapeño in half, remove all seeds and ribs, and finely mince (use rubber gloves to keep the pepper from coating your fingers).

2. Combine cherries, bell pepper, onion, lime juice, and basil and toss gently. Add as much of the jalapeño as your taste dictates. Add salt to taste.

3. Cover and leave at room temperature for 30 minutes before serving.

4.. Use ⅔ of the recipes ot marinate the steak. Serve the remaining ⅓ of the salsa on top of the cooked steak.

Summer Vegetable Grill

SEASON
Summer

PREPARATION TIME
20 minutes

SERVINGS
4 (1 cup each)

NUTRITION FACTS

calories	77
total fat	2.6 grams
saturated fat	0.4 grams
cholesterol	0 milligrams
sodium	4 milligrams
carbohydrate	10.1 grams
fiber	3.8 grams
protein	3.1 grams

SUPER SALAD: *romaine lettuce, mini mixed bell peppers, cherry tomatoes, and cucumbers*

INGREDIENTS

2 small Japanese eggplants

2 small zucchini

2 yellow crookneck squash

1 each small orange, red, and yellow bell peppers

1 teaspoon toasted sesame oil

1 tablespoon sesame seeds

Pepper blend, freshly ground, to taste

DIRECTIONS

1. Wash and cut eggplants, zucchini, and squash lengthwise. Peppers may be cut into quarters.

2. Brush cut-sides of vegetables with a small amount of sesame oil.

3. Preheat grill and place vegetables over high heat, cut-sides down.

4. Grill until vegetables are browned, but not blackened.

5. Turn vegetables over and grill 3-4 minutes until soft, but still crisp.

6. Serve topped with sesame seeds and freshly ground pepper blend.

WEEK 3

Week Three Plans

Week at a Glance

Day	Modules	Recipe	Super Salad	Side Dish(es)
1	Entrée	Scallops with French Sorrel Sauce	Purple leaf lettuce, blood oranges, and sunflower seeds	Spring Asparagus and Fennel Sauté
2	Main course	Ginger Orange Soup	Mixed color baby greens, raspberries, and avocado	Seeded flat bread
3	Entrée	Sea Bass with Macadamia Nut Pesto Sauce	Spinach, pear, and blackberries	Green Beans with Almonds and Roasted Red Bell Peppers
4	Main course	Country Tuna Pie	Shredded purple cabbage, sliced apples, and organic salad walnuts	None
5	Entrée	Beef and Cauliflower Stroganoff	Tricolor base with purple heirloom tomatoes and olives	Orange-Glazed Carrots and Parsnips
6	Free			
7	Entrée	Rainbow Chicken Salad	None	Cornbread

Day 1

BREAKFAST

+ Purple Passion Shake (recipe on page 159)
+ 1 slice toasted, whole-grain English muffin with 1 tablespoon peanut butter

LUNCH

+ Pita pocket with tomatoes, avocado, and sunflower sprouts

DINNER

+ Scallops with French Sorrel Sauce (recipe on page 160)
+ Spring Asparagus and Fennel Sauté (recipe on page 162)
+ Super Salad: purple leaf lettuce, blood oranges, and sunflower seeds with raspberry vinaigrette

Day 2

BREAKFAST

+ 1 cup whole-grain cereal
+ 1 cup soy milk
+ ½ cup raspberries
+ ½ cup orange juice

LUNCH

+ Super Salad: cottage cheese, pears, and almonds with raspberry vinaigrette

DINNER

+ Ginger-Orange Soup (recipe on page 163)
+ Super Salad: baby greens, raspberry, avocado, and bleu cheese with balsamic vinaigrette
+ 1 slice seeded flat bread

Day 3

BREAKFAST

+ 1 cup cooked organic oatmeal
+ ½ cup yogurt

A NEW WAY OF EATING

- ½ cup blueberries
- ½ banana

LUNCH
- 2 cups Ginger Orange Soup from the night before
- 1 seeded flat bread

DINNER
- Sea Bass with Macadamia Nut Pesto Sauce (recipe on page 164)
- Super Salad: baby spinach, pear, and blackberries with raspberry vinaigrette
- Green Beans with Almonds and Roasted Red Bell Peppers (recipe on page 166)

Day 4

BREAKFAST
- Strawberry Yogurt Breakfast Shake (recipe on page 121)
- 1 slice whole-wheat toast coated with 1 tablespoon fruit spread
- ½ cup grape juice

LUNCH
- Super Salad: one sliced hard-cooked egg, sliced beets, roasted yellow bell peppers, and lemon juice

DINNER
- Country Tuna Pie (recipe on page 167)
- Super Salad: shredded purple cabbage, sliced apples, organic salad walnuts, and sesame dressing

Day 5

BREAKFAST

+ Fruit Cup with Yogurt (recipe on page 129)
+ ½ whole-grain bagel with1 tablespoon cream cheese

LUNCH

+ Country Tuna Pie leftover from dinner

DINNER

+ Beef and Cauliflower Stroganoff (recipe on page 169)
+ Super Salad: tricolor base with purple heirloom tomatoes and olives
+ Orange-Glazed Carrots and Parsnips (recipe on page 170)

Day 6 or 7: Weekend

+ Rainbow Chicken Salad (recipe on page 171)
+ Cornbread (follow package directions)

Shopping Lists

TAN FOODS

cornmeal (organic)	seeded flat bread
macadamia nuts	whole-grain cereals
peanut butter	whole-grain English muffins
pita pockets	and bagels
pink lentils	whole-wheat bread
potatoes, russet	whole-wheat pastry flour

A NEW WAY OF EATING

WHITE FOODS

beef sirloin steak
(lean, 4 ounces per person)
cheddar cheese
chicken breast (skinless and
boneless, 4 ounces per
person)
chicken soup base
cottage cheese (low-fat)
eggs (organic)
feta cheese
Parmesan cheese

milk (low-fat)
sea scallops (large, 6 ounces per
person)
sea bass (6 ounces per person)
milk
soy
sour cream (fat-free)
tuna (1 can, water-packed)
sunflower seeds (raw)
yogurt (fat-free plain)

RAINBOW-COLORED FOODS

artichoke hearts (1 package,
frozen)
asparagus
avocados
baby greens
basil
beets
bell peppers (large, sweet, red,
yellow, and green)
blackberries
butternut squash
carrots
cauliflower
celery
cilantro

French sorrel
garlic
ginger root (fresh)
green beans
hearts of palm
lemons
limes
mushrooms
onions (yellow, purple, and sweet
Vidalia)
parsley
parsnips
pears
purple leaf lettuce
raspberries

roma tomatoes
rutabaga
scallions
shallots
sweet potato

tomato paste
tomatoes (3, or 1 can
    fire-roasted tomatoes)
yellow zucchini
zucchini

CONDIMENTS

baking powder
baking soda
balsamic vinegar
chicken broth (salt-free or
    low-sodium)
chili peppers (powdered)
honey
lemon-flavored olive oil

macadamia nut oil
olives (green and black whole)
orange juice
organic extra virgin olive oil
soy sauce
peppercorns
seasoned salt

Purple Passion Shake

NUTRITION FACTS

calories	476
total fat	3.8 grams
saturated fat	2 grams
cholesterol	4.5 milligrams
sodium	176 milligrams
carbohydrate	75.7 grams
fiber	4.2 grams
protein	34.5 grams

INGREDIENTS

1 cup nut or rice milk

¾ cup unsweetened berry juice

½ banana

⅓ cup blueberries

½ cup vanilla whey protein isolate powder (31 grams)

Scallops with French Sorrel Sauce

SEASON
Winter, early spring

PREPARATION TIME
10 minutes

SERVINGS
2

NUTRITION FACTS

calories	264
total fat	14.8 grams
saturated fat	1.9 grams
cholesterol	57 milligrams
sodium	274 milligrams
carbohydrate	4 grams
fiber	0 grams
protein	28.5 grams

Scallops

INGREDIENTS

12 ounces sea scallops

2 teaspoons lemon-flavored olive oil

blood orange slices

thyme sprigs, fresh

DIRECTIONS

1. Remove muscle along side of each scallop. Wash and pat dry.

2. Spray skillet well with cooking spray. (Scallops are delicate and stick easily.)

3. Add olive oil and heat.

4. Quickly sear scallops on each side.

5. Serve with ¼ cup French sorrel sauce drizzled over scallops.

6. Garnish with two blood orange slices and a sprig of fresh thyme.

PREPARATION TIME
10 minutes

SERVINGS
8 (¼ cup each)

NUTRITION FACTS

calories	84
total fat	9 grams
saturated fat	1.2 grams
cholesterol	0 milligrams
sodium	3 milligrams
carbohydrate	0.8 grams
fiber	0.2 grams
protein	0.1 grams

NOTE: *This sauce is also excellent over chicken, burgers, spaghetti squash, green beans, and whole-grain pasta. Sorrel leaves are brilliant green and provide a tangy and attractive sauce for fish or poultry. Sorrel is also an excellent digestive aid.*

INGREDIENTS

⅛ cup lemon juice

2 tablespoons lemon zest

1 cup fresh sorrel leaves, stems removed and chopped

⅓ cup extra virgin organic olive oil

DIRECTIONS

1. Grate or zest lemon and reserve.

2. Place all ingredients in food processor and blend until smooth.

Spring Asparagus and Fennel Sauté

SEASON
Spring

PREPARATION TIME
15 minutes

SERVINGS
4

NUTRITION FACTS

calories	67
total fat	2.5 grams
saturated fat	0.4 grams
cholesterol	0 milligrams
sodium	14 milligrams
carbohydrate	7.8 milligrams
fiber	3.3 grams
protein	3.3 grams

SUPER SALAD: *purple leaf lettuce, blood oranges, and sunflower seeds with raspberry vinaigrette*

INGREDIENTS

- **1 pound asparagus**
- **1 small fennel bulb**
- **2 teaspoons organic extra virgin olive oil**
- **¼ cup tarragon leaves, fresh**
- **¼ teaspoon pepper**

DIRECTIONS

1. Wash and trim asparagus, discarding woody stems.

2. Wash fennel and cut off stems and fine leaves; chop bulb into large chunks.

3. Heat oil in a wok and add vegetables and tarragon.

4. Sauté just until vegetables are tender-crisp

5. Sprinkle with pepper and serve.

Ginger Orange Soup

SEASON
Fall

PREPARATION TIME
20 minutes

SERVINGS
4 (2 cups each)

NUTRITION FACTS

calories	335
total fat	8.3 grams
saturated fat	1.1 grams
cholesterol	0 milligrams
sodium	547 milligrams
carbohydrate	50 grams
fiber	9.3 grams
protein	15.1 grams

SUPER SALAD: *mixed-colored baby greens, raspberries, avocado, and pine nuts with creamy ranch dressing*

INGREDIENTS

- 1 cup rutabaga, diced
- 1 teaspoon ginger root, peeled and grated
- ¼ cup flat, Italian parsley, chopped
- 1 cup carrots, peeled and diced
- 1 cup sweet potatoes, peeled and diced
- 1 large yellow bell pepper, diced
- 1 cup onion, diced
- 1 cup pink lentils
- ⅛ teaspoon cinnamon, ground
- 2 tablespoons organic extra virgin olive oil
- 1 tablespoon soup base, fat-free
- 2 cups water

DIRECTIONS

1. Lightly sauté rutabaga, ginger, parsley, carrots, sweet potatoes, bell pepper, and onion in a 3½-quart pressure cooker or stockpot until onions are translucent.

2. Add lentils, cinnamon, soup base, and water. Lock pressure cooker cover and raise pressure to first red ring, at 8 psi. Process 15 minutes.

3. If using a stock pot, bring soup to a boil, then add lid. Lower heat and simmer for 1 hour.

Sea Bass with Macadamia Nut Pesto Sauce

SEASON
All

PREPARATION TIME
20 minutes

SERVINGS
2 (6 ounces each)

NUTRITION FACTS

calories	282
total fat	8.6 grams
saturated fat	1.7 grams
cholesterol	70 milligrams
sodium	520 milligrams
carbohydrate	16.8 grams
fiber	3.3 grams
protein	34.3 grams

Sea Bass

INGREDIENTS

- ¾ cup green bell peppers, cut into quarters lengthwise for grilling
- 3 large zucchini, sliced into ½-inch slices lengthwise
- 1½ cups Italian Roma tomatoes, sliced lengthwise for grilling
- 12 ounces sea bass
- 2 teaspoons macadamia nut oil
- 1 tablespoon white-wine vinegar
- ½ teaspoon seasoned salt
- 1½ tablespoons lemon juice

DIRECTIONS

1. Lightly coat peppers, zucchini, and tomatoes with oil and grill until nicely browned. Place on a platter.

2. Place sea bass on grill and cook 3 minutes on one side. Turn over and grill 3 minutes on the other side.

3. Mix vinegar and salt with lemon juice and pour over vegetables.

4. Place sea bass on vegetables and spoon Macadamia Nut Pesto Sauce over fish.

PREPARATION TIME
15 minutes

SERVINGS
10 (2 tablespoons each)

NUTRITION FACTS
calories	201
total fat	21.1 grams
saturated fat	3.2 grams
cholesterol	0 milligrams
sodium	92 milligrams
carbohydrate	1.5 grams
fiber	0.8 grams
protein	1.2 grams

NOTE: *This sauce is also excellent over chicken, spaghetti squash, green beans, or whole-grain pasta.*

Macadamia Nut Pesto Sauce

INGREDIENTS

½ cup macadamia nuts

¾ cup fresh basil leaves

½ cup parsley, chopped

1 tablespoon garlic, minced

¾ cup macadamia nut oil

½ teaspoon seasoned salt

1 tablespoon Parmesan cheese, grated

DIRECTIONS

1. Place all ingredients in food processor and blend until smooth.

2. Chill or freeze leftover sauce.

Green Beans with Almonds and Roasted Red Bell Peppers

SEASON
Spring and summer

PREPARATION TIME
25 minutes

SERVINGS
4 (1 cup each)

NUTRITION FACTS

calories	207
total fat	15.7 grams
saturated fat	1.5 grams
cholesterol	0 milligrams
sodium	154 milligrams
carbohydrate	11.6 grams
fiber	4.4 grams
protein	4.9 grams

SUPER SALAD: *baby spinach leaves, pears, and blackberries with raspberry vinaigrette*

INGREDIENTS

- ¾ cup sliced raw almonds
- 12 ounces green beans
- 1 teaspoon minced garlic
- ½ cup red bell pepper, diced
- 1½ teaspoons organic extra virgin olive oil
- ¼ teaspoon salt

DIRECTIONS

1. Toast almonds by spreading them on cookie sheet in a 350°F oven for 8 to 10 minutes. Remove and set aside.

2. Wash and trim ends from green beans. Place in steamer basket and steam 20 minutes or just until tender, but still bright green. Shock with cold water to stop cooking. Drain and set aside.

3. Lightly sauté garlic and peppers in olive oil. Add salt and green beans and toss to mix.

4. Place each serving in a side dish and sprinkle with toasted almonds.

Country Tuna Pie

SEASON
Summer

PREPARATION TIME
15 minutes

SERVINGS
4 (2 cups each)

NUTRITION FACTS
calories 272
total fat 10 grams
saturated fat 3.3 grams
cholesterol 132 milligrams
sodium 474 milligrams
carbohydrate 23.1 grams
fiber 1.5 grams
protein 22.9 grams

NOTE: *A lower-fat, lower-calorie alternative can be made by using leftover garlic mashed potatoes to cover the tuna filling.*

INGREDIENTS

- 1 can tuna (6 ounces), water-packed
- ¼ cup green onion, diced
- ⅓ cup celery, diced
- ½ cup carrots, diced
- 1 large potato, diced
- 1 tablespoon organic olive oil
- 1 tablespoon arrowroot or flour
- 1 cup chicken broth, fat-free, low-sodium
- ¼ cup flat, Italian parsley, diced
- ¼ cup roasted red bell pepper, minced
- ¼ cup cheddar cheese, shredded
- Easy Oil crust (see recipe on page 168)

DIRECTIONS

1. Drain tuna; reserve liquid and set aside.
2. Sauté green onion, celery, carrots, and potatoes in olive oil until tender.
3. Sprinkle arrowroot or flour over oil and vegetables. Stir to blend.
4. Add chicken broth and continue to stir until thickened.
5. Stir in flaked tuna, parsley, pepper, and cheese.
6. Blend well and turn into two small casserole dishes.
7. Cover with Easy Oil Crust, leaving two vent holes.
8. Bake in 350°F oven for 45 minutes or until knife inserted in center comes out clean.
9. Let stand 10 minutes before serving.

SUGGESTION: *Leftover tuna pie makes a great lunch the next day.*

RECIPE CONTINUES

NUTRITION FACTS

calories	232
total fat	14.2 grams
saturated fat	1.3 grams
cholesterol	0 milligrams
sodium	149 milligrams
carbohydrate	21.8 grams
fiber	3.7 grams
protein	4.1 grams

Easy Oil Crust

INGREDIENTS

1 cup whole-wheat pastry flour

¼ teaspoon salt

¼ cup organic walnut or macadamia nut oil

2 tablespoons cold water

DIRECTIONS

1. Stir flour and salt in a bowl.

2. Combine oil with water and add to flour and salt. Mix with a fork.

3. Form into two balls with your hands and let sit covered with a cloth for 5 minutes.

4. Roll out between sheets of waxed paper.

5. Cover tuna and vegetable filling with crusts and bake for 10 to 12 minutes at 400° F.

Beef and Cauliflower Stroganoff

SEASON
All

PREPARATION TIME
30 minutes

SERVINGS
4 (4 ounces beef each)

NUTRITION FACTS

calories	316
total fat	13.3 grams
saturated fat	4.2 grams
cholesterol	74 milligrams
sodium	559 milligrams
carbohydrate	20.7 grams
fiber	4 grams
protein	28.3 grams

SUPER SALAD: *tricolor base (Belgian endive, arugula, radicchio), purple heirloom tomatoes, and olives with red wine vinaigrette*

INGREDIENTS

- 1 tablespoon organic olive oil
- 1 pound top sirloin or rib eye steak, cut into bite-sized pieces
- 2 small green zucchini, julienne
- 1 large red bell pepper, julienne
- ½ cup beef broth, fat-free and low-sodium
- 2 ounces of cognac or sherry
- ½ teaspoon seasoned salt
- 1 teaspoon cumin, ground
- ¼ teaspoon pepper (or to taste), freshly ground
- 1 tablespoon ketchup, low-sodium
- ½ tablespoon tomato paste
- 1 cup mushrooms, sliced
- 1 large cauliflower (approximately 4 cups)
- 1 cup nonfat sour cream

DIRECTIONS

1. In nonstick frying pan, heat olive oil, add steak pieces, and cook until golden-brown and fully cooked. Set aside. (Steak pieces can also be grilled or roasted.)

2. In the same frying pan, sauté the zucchini and bell pepper. Set aside.

3. Add beef broth, cognac or sherry, salt, cumin, pepper, ketchup, and tomato paste.

4. Add mushrooms, meat, and sautéed zucchini and red pepper. Steam 15 minutes.

5. Meanwhile, steam cauliflower and cut into bite-sized pieces (can be replaced with whole-grain pasta).

6. Add nonfat sour cream before serving.

Orange-Glazed Carrots and Parsnips

SEASON
All

PREPARATION TIME
10 minutes

SERVINGS
2 (1 cup each)

NUTRITION FACTS
calories 141
total fat 2.3 grams
saturated fat 1.2 grams
cholesterol 5 milligrams
sodium 277 milligrams
carbohydrate 27.2 grams
fiber 5.8 grams
protein 2.7 grams

INGREDIENTS

1 cup parsnips

1 cup carrots

½ cup onion, sliced

1 tablespoon ginger root, grated

1 teaspoon unsalted butter

2 teaspoons orange juice

1 tablespoon soy sauce, low-sodium

1 teaspoon honey

¼ teaspoon black pepper, freshly ground

DIRECTIONS

1. Peel carrots and parsnips and slice both diagonally; carrots in ⅛-inch slices and parsnips in ¼-inch slices.

2. Sauté the onion slices in butter until limp and add carrots and ginger, stirring to coat.

3. Add orange juice and soy sauce and cook over low heat approximately 8 minutes.

4. Add parsnips, honey, and pepper.

5. Cover and cook until sauce has a nice, syrupy consistency.

Rainbow Chicken Salad

SEASON
Summer

PREPARATION TIME
20 minutes

SERVINGS
4 (4 ounces chicken each)

NUTRITION FACTS
calories	356
total fat	17 grams
saturated fat	4.8 grams
cholesterol	82 milligrams
sodium	805 milligrams
carbohydrate	15.8 grams
fiber	5.5 grams
protein	33.5 grams

INGREDIENTS

- 2 chicken breasts, boneless, skinless, approximately 16 ounces total
- 8 cups mixed baby greens with purple radicchio
- 6 kalamata olives, cut in quarters
- 6 green olives, cut in quarters
- 3 stalks hearts of palm, sliced
- 1 large cooked and chilled beet, diced
- 1 small yellow zucchini, diced
- ½ cup red bell pepper, diced
- ½ cup yellow bell pepper, diced
- ½ cup artichoke hearts (4 ounces), large dice
- 2 tablespoons organic olive oil
- 1 tablespoon balsamic vinegar
- ½ teaspoon seasoned salt
- ¼ teaspoon (or to taste) black pepper, freshly ground
- ½ cup feta cheese

DIRECTIONS

1. In a frying pan coated with cooking spray, brown chicken breasts, cooking 3–4 minutes per side or until golden-brown and fully cooked. Set aside to cool and then slice in strips. (Chicken can be grilled or roasted.)

2. In a large salad bowl, mix greens and radicchio and add olives, hearts of palm, beet, zucchini, peppers, and artichoke hearts.

3. In a separate bowl, mix olive oil, balsamic vinegar, salt, and black pepper

4. Pour salad dressing over salad and toss well.

5. Divide into four portions on salad plates.

6. Add feta cheese and sliced chicken.

Step Three: Fix Your Meals

171

WEEK 4

Week Four Plans

Week at a Glance

Day	Modules	Recipe	Super Salad	Side Dish(es)
1	Entrée	Shrimp with Sun-Dried Tomato Sauce	Purple radicchio, orange slices, feta cheese, and organic pecans	Corn on the cob
2	Main course	Purple Borscht Soup with Beef	Romaine lettuce, asparagus, pimiento, and sesame seeds	Asiago cheese bread
3	Entrée	Chicken Basmati Rice with Garden Vegetables and Herbs	None	Fruit Cup with Yogurt
4	Main course	Couscous and Lentils	Mesclun with sliced red and yellow pears	Stir-Fried Vegetables with Toasted Cashews
5	Entrée	Spring Halibut Sauté with Vegetables and Linguine	Bibb lettuce cup, tangerine segments, and pimiento strips	Butternut Squash and Kale Sauté
6	Free			
7	Entrée	Grilled Swordfish with Chipotle Salsa	Classic Caesar Salad	Steamed asparagus, lemon, and tarragon

Day 1

BREAKFAST
* 1 cup whole-grain cereal
* 1 cup vanilla yogurt
* ½ cup peaches, sliced
* ½ cup carrot juice

LUNCH
* Rainbow Chicken Salad (recipe on page 171)
* Small bunch of grapes

DINNER
* Shrimp with Sun-Dried Tomato Sauce (recipe on page 180)
* Super Salad: purple radicchio, orange slices, feta cheese, and organic pecans.
* Corn-on-the-cob

Day 2

BREAKFAST
* Vanilla Peach Shake (recipe on page 181)
* ½ whole-grain bagel with almond butter
* ½ cup berries

LUNCH
* Small Super Salad with cottage cheese
* 4 small whole-grain crackers

DINNER
* Purple Borscht Soup with Beef (recipe on page 182)

- Super Salad: romaine lettuce, asparagus, pimiento, and sesame seeds
- Asiago cheese bread

Day 3

BREAKFAST
- Hard-boiled egg
- Whole-grain toast
- ½ cup cranberry juice
- Small orange

LUNCH
- Purple Borscht Soup with Beef from dinner

DINNER
- Chicken Basmati Rice with Garden Vegetables and Herbs (recipe on page 183)
- Fruit Cup with Yogurt (recipe on page 129)

Day 4

BREAKFAST
- Raspberry Parfait Shake (recipe on page 185)
- Whole-grain English muffin with toasted sesame butter
- Small orange

LUNCH
- Chicken Basmati Rice with Garden Vegetables and Herbs from dinner

DINNER

- Couscous and Lentils (recipe on page 186)
- Stir-Fried Vegetables with Toasted Cashews (recipe on page 187)
- Super Salad: mesclun with sliced red and yellow pears

Day 5

BREAKFAST

- Brazilian Mocha Shake (recipe on page 188)
- Whole-grain toast with fruit spread
- ½ apricot

LUNCH

- Pita pocket with prepared hummus, mesclun, and cucumber slices

DINNER

- Spring Halibut Sauté with Vegetables and Linguini (recipe on page 189)
- Butternut Squash and Kale Sauté (recipe on page 190)
- Super Salad: Bibb lettuce cup, tangerine segments, and pimiento strips

Day 6 or 7: Weekend

BREAKFAST

- Vegetable Omelet (recipe on page 191)
- Whole Wheat Toast with Fruit Spread (recipe on page 191)
- Fruit Plate for Two (recipe on page 192)

DINNER

- Grilled Swordfish with Chipotle Salsa (recipe on page 193)
- Super Salad: Classic Caesar Salad (recipe on page 195)
- Steamed Asparagus with Lemon and Tarragon (recipe on page 196)

Shopping Lists

TAN FOODS

- arrowroot
- basmati rice (brown)
- basmati rice mix with dried vegetables
- cashews, organic
- couscous (golden), organic
- croutons (plain sourdough)
- English muffins and bagels
- garbanzo beans (small can)
- lentils (pink)
- organic pecans
- spinach and olive linguini
- whey protein (vanilla, chocolate, strawberry)
- whole-grain bread
- yogurt, vanilla

WHITE FOODS

- almond or organic oat milk
- ancolvies
- beef chuck
- chicken breast, boneless and skinless
- cottage cheese, low fat
- eggs
- feta cheese with basil and sun-dried tomatoes
- halibut steaks, 8 ounces
- milk, low-fat
- Parmesan cheese
- shrimp, large, 1 pound
- swordfish, 8 ounces
- yogurt, plain

Rainbow-Colored Foods

- artichoke hearts, bottled or frozen
- asparagus
- bananas
- basil, fresh
- beets
- bell peppers, red, yellow, and orange
- Bibb lettuce
- blueberries
- broccoli
- bok-choy
- butternut squash, small
- cabbage, purple
- cantaloupe
- carrots
- cherry tomatoes
- chipotle chilis
- cilantro
- fruit juice, sweetened
- garlic
- ginger root, fresh
- jam, 100% fruit
- kale leaves, dark green
- lemons
- limes
- onions, pearl
- onions, purple and yellow
- oranges
- oregano, fresh
- parsley
- parsnips
- peaches
- pimientos or roasted bell peppers, bottled
- radicchio
- raspberries
- red-skinned potatoes
- romaine
- scallions (green onions)
- shiitake mushrooms
- spring greens mix
- tangerines or mandarin oranges
- tomatillos
- tomatoes
- tomatoes, sun-dried
- turnips
- watercress
- watermelon

Condiments

- chicken broth, fat-free, low-sodium
- chili pepper flakes
- chili powder
- chili verde salsa
- chipotle chili powder (if not using fresh)
- cumin, powdered
- fish sauce
- Italian herb blend
- nutmeg
- organic extra virgin olive oil
- olives, chopped, small can
- red pepper flakes, dried
- red wine vinegar
- soup base, fat-free chicken, beef, and vegetable
- tomato paste
- white wine
- white wine vinegar
- Worcestershire sauce

Shrimp with Sun-Dried Tomato Sauce

SEASON
All

PREPARATION TIME
45 minutes

SERVINGS
2

SUPER SALAD: *purple radicchio, orange slices, feta cheese, and organic pecans with bottled sesame ginger dressing*

INGREDIENTS

- **¼ cup sun-dried tomatoes**
- **½ cup boiling water**
- **2 teaspoons Worcestershire sauce**
- **2 teaspoons lemon juice**
- **1 tablespoon organic extra virgin olive oil**
- **½ teaspoon garlic, crushed**
- **¼ teaspoon dried chili pepper flakes**
- **1 teaspoon fresh ginger root, grated**
- **¾ teaspoon chili powder**
- **¼ teaspoon black pepper**
- **1 tablespoon butter**
- **1 tablespoon cilantro, chopped**
- **1 pound large shrimp, peeled**

DIRECTIONS

1. Heat oven to 425°F.

2. In a small bowl, combine sun-dried tomatoes and boiling water. Let sit 20 minutes.

3. Place sun-dried tomatoes and their soaking liquid in blender. Add Worcestershire sauce, lemon juice, and salt and blend to a course purée.

4. In a medium saucepan, heat oil over low heat. Add garlic, dried pepper flakes, and ginger and cook, stirring 3 minutes.

5. Add chili powder and black pepper and cook, stirring 30 seconds longer. Add butter and melt.

6. Remove pan from heat and stir in tomato mixture. Add shrimp and stir to combine.

7. Place shrimp and sauce in a baking dish in an even layer. Bake until just done, approximately 11 minutes.

Vanilla Peach Shake

NUTRITION FACTS

calories	378
total fat	2.4 grams
saturated fat	1.3 grams
cholesterol	10 milligrams
sodium	128 milligrams
carbohydrate	55.6 grams
fiber	2.2 grams
protein	33.3 grams

INGREDIENTS

1 cup orange juice

1 whole peach, sliced, or ½ cup frozen peach slices

½ cup vanilla yogurt, low-fat

½ cup vanilla whey protein isolate powder (31 grams)

Purple Borscht Soup with Beef

SEASON
Cool

PREPARATION TIME
20 minutes to prepare vegetables; 15 minutes in a pressure cooker; 1 hour in conventional pot

SERVINGS
4

NUTRITION FACTS

calories	286
total fat	5.4 grams
saturated fat	1.8 grams
cholesterol	36 milligrams
sodium	707 milligrams
carbohydrate	40.8 grams
fiber	10.5 grams
protein	18.4 grams

SUPER SALAD: *romaine lettuce, asparagus, pimiento, and sesame seeds with bottled, spicy miso dressing*

For the vegetarian version of this soup, eliminate beef and beef broth. Use vegetable broth or soup base and add 2 tablespoons organic olive oil, then prepare the same way.

INGREDIENTS

- **½ pound beef chuck, cut into small chunks**
- **½ cup turnips, large dice**
- **½ cup parsnips, large dice**
- **1 pound red-skinned potatoes, scrubbed**
- **2 cups carrots, peeled, large dice**
- **1 cup baby pearl onions, peeled**
- **3 cups beets, large dice**
- **2 tablespoons tomato paste**
- **2 tablespoons red wine vinegar**
- **1 tablespoon soup base, fat-free**
- **1 quart boiling water**
- **3 cups purple cabbage, shredded or medium dice**

DIRECTIONS

1. Coat a 3½-quart pressure cooker with cooking spray. Add beef and brown it.

2. Add turnips, parsnips, potatoes, carrots, onions, beets, tomato paste, vinegar, soup base, and boiling water.

3. Process in a pressure cooker set at first red ring (8 psi) for 15 minutes. Remove from heat and let pressure drop naturally. Alternately, cook in a covered stockpot for 1 hour.

4. When soup is done, remove lid and add cabbage. Simmer without lid for 5–6 minutes until cabbage is tender.

Chicken Basmati Rice
with Garden Vegetables and Herbs

This salad also can be served hot. Steam spinach in a large wok; add artichoke hearts and garbanzo beans just to warm them through. Add chicken pieces and dressing. Serve over warm basmati rice/vegetable blend.

SEASON
All

PREPARATION TIME
45 minutes (including time to cook rice)

SERVINGS
2

NUTRITION FACTS
(includes basmati rice below)
calories	461
total fat	15.7 grams
saturated fat	2.3 grams
cholesterol	65 milligrams
sodium	278 milligrams
carbohydrate	45.2 grams
fiber	8.1 grams
protein	34.5 grams

Chicken

INGREDIENTS

- **4 tablespoons balsamic vinegar**
- **2 tablespoons organic extra virgin olive oil**
- **1 teaspoon Italian herbs**
- **¼ teaspoon black pepper, freshly ground**
- **8 ounces chicken breast, skinless and boneless**
- **4 cups spring greens salad mix or spinach**
- **⅔ cup cooked basmati rice and vegetable mix (see recipe on p. 184)**
- **½ cup artichoke hearts, bottled and water-packed**
- **1 cup garbanzo beans (chickpeas), cooked**

DIRECTIONS

1. Mix balsamic vinegar, olive oil, Italian herbs, and black pepper and let sit.

2. Prepare basmati rice (recipe below).

3. Grill, broil, or steam chicken breasts.

4. Assemble salad according to Super Salad Savvy (see Step Three, page 78) and top with dressing.

(RECIPE CONTINUES)

Basmati Rice with Vegetables and Herbs

INGREDIENTS

- **2 cups water**
- **1 cup basmati rice mixed with dried vegetables**
- **1 teaspoon organic olive oil**
- **1 teaspoon soup base, fat-free**
- **2 teaspoons fresh oregano, minced**

DIRECTIONS

1. In heavy saucepan, combine water, rice, oil, soup base, and oregano.

2. Bring mixture to boil, stir to blend, reduce heat, and cover.

3. Simmer 15 minutes. Remove from heat and let rest 5 minutes.

4. Fluff with a fork and serve.

Raspberry Parfait Shake

NUTRITION FACTS

calories	345
total fat	1.1 grams
saturated fat	0.3 grams
cholesterol	10.5 milligrams
sodium	94 milligrams
carbohydrate	53.4 grams
fiber	6.8 grams
protein	30.1 grams

INGREDIENTS

¾ cup raspberries

¼ cup vanilla yogurt, low-fat

1 cup pineapple juice

½ cup strawberry whey protein isolate powder (31 grams)

Couscous and Lentils

SEASON
Summer

PREPARATION TIME
40 to 45 minutes

SERVINGS
6 Super Salads

NUTRITION FACTS
calories 305
total fat 13.4 grams
saturated fat 3.4 grams
cholesterol 11 milligrams
sodium 379 milligrams
carbohydrate 35.7 grams
fiber 4 grams
protein 10.2 grams

INGREDIENTS

- ½ cup pink lentils
- ½ teaspoon salt
- ¼ cup organic extra virgin olive oil
- 1¼ cups water
- 1 cup organic couscous
- ½ cup lemon juice
- 3 tablespoons red wine vinegar
- 2 garlic cloves, mashed into a paste
- 4 scallions, minced (can substitute with one-half red onion)
- 2 cups watercress, packed leaves
- ½ cup cherry tomatoes, cut into halves
- ½ cup olives, diced
- ¼ teaspoon black pepper, freshly ground
- ½ cup feta cheese with basil and sun-dried tomatoes, crumbled

DIRECTIONS

1. Place lentils in a medium saucepan and add enough water to cover by 2 inches.

2. Bring water to boil, add half the salt (¼ teaspoon) and 1 tablespoon of olive oil.

3. Reduce heat and simmer until lentils are tender, approximately 40 to 45 minutes. Drain, rinse under cold water, and place in mixing bowl.

4. To prepare couscous, bring 1¼ cups water and remaining salt to a boil. Stir in couscous, remove from heat, and cover tightly.

5. Let stand until couscous has absorbed the water, approximately 10 minutes. Fluff with a fork and combine with lentils.

6. Mix lemon juice, vinegar, remaining olive oil, and garlic. Pour over lentils and couscous and mix well. Cover and chill.

7. Mix scallions, watercress, tomatoes, olives, and pepper. Cover and chill.

8. Arrange a bed of the watercress mixture on a salad plate, place 1 cup of the lentil and couscous mixture over the greens, and sprinkle feta cheese on top.

Stir-Fried Vegetables with Toasted Cashews

SEASON
Summer

PREPARATION TIME
25 minutes

SERVINGS
4

NUTRITION FACTS
calories 60
total fat 2.5 grams
saturated fat 0.4 grams
cholesterol 0 milligrams
sodium 3 milligrams
carbohydrate 6.2 grams
fiber 2.6 grams
protein 3 grams

SUPER SALAD: *mesclun with sliced red and yellow pears and bottled poppy seed dressing*

INGREDIENTS

- **3 tablespoons chicken broth, fat-free and low-sodium**
- **1 tablespoon arrowroot**
- **1 teaspoon organic olive oil**
- **⅓ cup organic cashew nuts, raw**
- **pinch red pepper flakes, dried**
- **2 teaspoons sesame oil**
- **1 cup shiitake mushrooms, fresh (rehydrate if using dried)**
- **¼ cup scallions, green tops finely chopped and white bulbs coarsely chopped**
- **1 teaspoon garlic, mashed or pressed**
- **2 cups broccoli, cut into small flowerets**
- **2 cups Chinese cabbage (bok choy), chopped**
- **½ cup red bell peppers, sliced into strips**

DIRECTIONS

1. In a small bowl, combine 1 tablespoon of the broth with arrowroot and set aside.

2. In a wok, heat olive oil over moderately high heat. Add cashews and cook, continuously stirring, until browned, 1–2 minutes. Transfer nuts to a medium bowl and add red pepper flakes.

3. In the wok, heat 1 teaspoon of the sesame oil. Add mushrooms and cook until golden brown, approximately 5 minutes. Transfer to a bowl with cashews and stir in scallion green tops.

4. Heat the remaining teaspoon of sesame oil in the wok, add scallion bulbs and garlic and cook 30 seconds. Add broccoli and cook, stirring, for 1 minute. Add cabbage and bell peppers and cook until cabbage wilts, approximately 2 minutes.

5. Add remaining broth, broth and arrowroot mixture, and fish sauce. Heat through and serve.

Brazilian Mocha Shake

NUTRITION FACTS

calories	338
total fat	3.4 grams
saturated fat	2 grams
cholesterol	4.5 milligrams
sodium	169 milligrams
carbohydrate	43.4 grams
fiber	2.7 grams
protein	34.4 grams

INGREDIENTS

1 teaspoon instant coffee

2 cups almond or organic oat milk

½ cup banana, sliced

½ cup chocolate whey protein isolate powder (31 grams)

Spring Halibut Sauté with Vegetables and Linguini

SEASON
Spring

PREPARATION TIME
30 minutes

SERVINGS
2

NUTRITION FACTS
calories 436
total fat 6.5 grams
saturated fat 1.1 grams
cholesterol 48 milligrams
sodium 168 milligrams
carbohydrate 56.8 grams
fiber 7.4 grams
protein 37.7 grams

INGREDIENTS

- 8 ounces halibut steak
- 1 teaspoon organic extra virgin olive oil
- 8 ounces asparagus, trimmed and cut on the diagonal
- ½ cup mushrooms
- ¼ cup purple onions, sliced into rings
- 1 cup red or orange bell peppers, cut into strips
- 1 teaspoon thyme, fresh
- 4 ounces dry, white wine
- 1 cup chicken broth, fat-free and low-sodium
- 2 cups cooked spinach and chive linguine (prepared according to package directions)
- 2 sprigs fresh thyme
- ¼ cup cilantro, chopped

DIRECTIONS

1. In a skillet coated with cooking spray, lightly brown halibut on both sides. (The fish also can be grilled, and the vegetables and pasta can be prepared separately.) Set aside.

2. In the same pan or in a wok, add olive oil and lightly sauté asparagus, mushrooms, onion rings, and peppers.

3. Nestle halibut among the vegetables. Add thyme, wine, and chicken broth.

4. Reduce heat and simmer approximately 7 minutes until vegetables are tender but crisp, and halibut flakes when pierced with a fork. Remove halibut and place on plates. Add pasta to vegetables and their juices. Toss to combine. Sprinkle cilantro on top.

5. Serve halibut beside the pasta-and-vegetable combination. Garnish with sprigs of fresh thyme.

Butternut Squash and Kale Sauté

SEASON
All

PREPARATION TIME
20 minutes

SERVINGS
4

NUTRITION FACTS
calories 109
total fat 4.2 grams
saturated fat 0.8 grams
cholesterol 0 milligrams
sodium 32 milligrams
carbohydrate 14.5 grams
fiber 2.9 grams
protein 3.4 grams

SUPER SALAD: *Bibb lettuce cup, tangerine segments, and pimiento strips with Lime Ginger Dressing (recipe on page 94)*

INGREDIENTS

- 1½ teaspoons garlic, crushed or pressed
- 1 cup onions, diced
- 1 tablespoon organic olive oil
- 2 cups butternut squash, diced
- ½ cup fresh basil, chopped
- 1 cup dark green kale, chopped
- 2 teaspoons white wine vinegar
- 1 teaspoon nutmeg, ground

DIRECTIONS

1. In a wok, sauté garlic and onions in olive oil. Add butternut squash, cover, and cook for 7 minutes or until squash is soft, but still firm.

2. Add basil and kale. Cover and steam 10 minutes until kale is wilted and squash is soft.

3. Add vinegar and nutmeg. Toss and serve.

Vegetable Omelet

SEASON
Summer

PREPARATION TIME
15 minutes

SERVINGS
2

NUTRITION FACTS
calories 151
total fat 8.7 grams
saturated fat 2.4 grams
cholesterol 259 milligrams
sodium 281 milligrams
carbohydrate 8.9 grams
fiber 2.3 grams
protein 9.2 grams

INGREDIENTS

1 teaspoon organic olive oil, salad oil, or cooking oil

1 cup combination red, orange, and yellow bell peppers, diced

⅓ cup onions, diced

¼ cup basil, fresh, chopped

¼ teaspoon black pepper

¼ teaspoon seasoned salt

4 eggs

2 tablespoons 2%-fat milk

1 cup mixed baby greens or arugula

DIRECTIONS

1. In a nonstick sauté pan, cook bell peppers, onions, and basil in oil until limp.

2. In a separate bowl, beat eggs and milk together.

3. Pour egg mixture over vegetables.

4. As egg mixture cooks around the edge of the pan, gently lift the edge to allow the uncooked egg to run underneath.

5. When nearly done, gently flip the omelet.

6. Season with salt and pepper.

7. Serve over greens or arugula and top with green chili salsa.

Whole Wheat Toast with Fruit Spread

SEASON
All

PREPARATION TIME
3 minutes

SERVINGS
1

NUTRITION FACTS
calories 85
total fat 1.1 grams
saturated fat 0.2 grams
cholesterol 0 milligrams
sodium 139 milligrams
carbohydrate 16.2 grams
fiber 1.8 grams
protein 2.5 grams

INGREDIENTS

1 teaspoon natural fruit spread, fruit juice, sweetened

1 slice whole-grain bread, small bagel, or ½ English muffin, toasted

Step Three: Fix Your Meals

Fruit Plate for Two

SEASON
Summer

PREPARATION TIME
12 minutes

SERVINGS
2

NUTRITION FACTS
calories 160
total fat 1.5 grams
saturated fat 0.6 grams
cholesterol 3 milligrams
sodium 56 milligrams
carbohydrate 32.2 grams
fiber 3.5 grams
protein 4.8 grams

INGREDIENTS

1½ cups melon mix and cantaloupe

1 cup blueberries

¼ cup peaches

½ cup vanilla yogurt, low-fat

½ teaspoon cinnamon or nutmeg, grated

DIRECTIONS

1. Cut up large pieces of fruit, removing rind or skin.

2. Divide into two bowls and top with yogurt. Sprinkle with cinnamon or nutmeg.

Grilled Swordfish with Chipotle Salsa

PREPARATION TIME
25 minutes for salsa
preparation plus grilling time

NUTRITION FACTS
for swordfish

calories	131
total fat	4.5
saturated fat	1.2 grams
cholesterol	44 milligrams
sodium	102 milligrams
carbohydrate	0 grams
fiber	0 grams
protein	22.5 grams

Swordfish

INGREDIENTS

8 ounces swordfish steaks

DIRECTIONS

1. Wash steaks and pat dry.

2. Marinate steaks in chipotle sauce (recipe follows) at least 1 hour and overnight, if possible.

3. Place on hot grill and cook approximately 5 to 6 minutes on each side.

4. Serve with additional chipotle sauce and Basmati Rice with Vegetables and Herbs (recipe on page 184).

(RECIPE CONTINUES)

Chipotle Salsa

SERVINGS
2 (4 ounces swordfish and
¼ cup salsa each)

NUTRITION FACTS
for chipotle sauce
calories 34
total fat 0.7 grams
saturated fat 0.1 grams
cholesterol 0 milligrams
sodium 200 milligrams
carbohydrate 5.9 grams
fiber 1.7 grams
protein 1 gram

INGREDIENTS

10 medium tomatillos, diced

2 cups tomatoes, peeled and diced (skins can be removed easily by plunging tomatoes into boiling water for 15 seconds and then running them under cold water)

½ cup onion, fine dice

1 clove garlic, minced or pressed

¼ ounce chipotle pepper (or ½ teaspoon powdered chipotle pepper)

1 teaspoon seasoned salt

½ cup cilantro, chopped

1 teaspoon cumin, ground

DIRECTIONS

1. Add all ingredients except cilantro to 2-quart pot.

2. Simmer 20 minutes, until tomatillos and tomatoes are soft.

3. Cool, add cilantro, and reserve.

Super Salad: Classic Caesar Salad

SEASON
All

PREPARATION TIME
15 minutes

SERVINGS
2 (3 cups each)

NUTRITION FACTS
for salad with anchovies

calories	330
total fat	22.3 grams
saturated fat	5.4 grams
cholesterol	120 milligrams
sodium	898 milligrams
carbohydrate	17.8 grams
fiber	2.7 grams
protein	14.4 grams

NUTRITION FACTS
for salad without anchovies

calories	300
total fat	20.8 grams
saturated fat	5.1 grams
cholesterol	107 milligrams
sodium	348 milligrams
carbohydrate	17.8 grams
fiber	2.7 grams
protein	10.1 grams

NOTE: *A classic Caesar salad is hard to beat. Most so-called Caesar salads don't even come close to this one. But this salad derives 60 percent of its calories from fat and contains a significant amount of sodium. So enjoy it just once in a while, and make sure everything else you eat during the day is low in both fat and salt.*

INGREDIENTS

- **6 anchovy fillets, mashed (optional)**
- **2 teaspoons garlic, mashed**
- **¼ cup lemon juice**
- **1 fresh egg yolk, beaten well**
- **2 tablespoons organic extra virgin olive oil, high-quality**
- **1 teaspoon black pepper, fresh, coarse ground**
- **6 ounces crisp romaine leaves (approximately 10 leaves), torn into bite-sized pieces**
- **1 cup plain sourdough bread croutons**
- **¼ cup Parmesan cheese, freshly grated**

DIRECTIONS

1. If using anchovies, drain oil from fillets and mash in a mortar and pestle (or in the bottom of a wooden salad bowl).

2. Add garlic and mash into anchovies. Place in a wooden salad bowl, if mixture was mashed using a mortar and pestle.

3. Add lemon juice to the anchovy and garlic mixture, add 1 egg yolk; mix thoroughly to "cook" the yolk.

4. Add the olive oil and pepper, mix thoroughly.

5. Add romaine lettuce and croutons and toss to mix well.

6. Garnish with Parmesan and serve immediately.

Steamed Asparagus with Tarragon and Lemon

SEASON
Spring

PREPARATION TIME
10 minutes

SERVINGS
2 (¾ cups each)

NUTRITION FACTS
calories 38
total fat 0.2 grams
saturated fat 0 grams
cholesterol 0 milligrams
sodium 197 milligrams
carbohydrate 6.4 grams
fiber 2.3 grams
protein 2.5 grams

INGREDIENTS

1½ cups fresh asparagus, washed, woody stem parts removed and cut on the diagonal into 1-inch slices

2 4-inch sprigs of fresh tarragon, leaves stripped from stems and coarsely chopped

⅛ cup lemon juice

¼ teaspoon real salt

¼ teaspoon freshly ground black pepper

DIRECTIONS

1. Place asparagus slices in a steamer basket.

2. Sprinkle the tarragon over the asparagus.

3. Cover and steam for 8 to 19 minutes until tender crisp and still bright green.

4. Stir salt and pepper into lemon juice.

5. Serve asparagus and tarragon with lemon mixture drizzled over it.

CHAPTER SEVEN

Step Four: Savor Your Food

TAKE TIME to slow down and enjoy your meals because it's one of the most important things you can do to improve your health. Seems too simple to be true, doesn't it? Nevertheless, new scientific evidence confirms that your ability to extract the maximum nutritional value from your meals will be enhanced by savoring every bite.

Feast First with Your Eyes

Take a moment to check out what's before you—the people you're dining with, the table setting, and the food you're about to enjoy. In other words, feast first with your eyes. What you see and smell wafting from the dishes before you should get your digestive juices flowing and engage your mind to anticipate a tasty experience. If what you see on your plate or your expectation of what it will taste like doesn't grab your interest and make you smile, then you're eating in a default mode and one that's far too common in today's world. If you believe you've been eating with the wrong attitude, ask yourself these questions. Are you eating out of habit or boredom? To counter an emotion? Out of obligation—that is, because there's food in front of you?

Be critical of your eating behavior, because what you eat and how you eat it determines how efficiently you can metabolize your food, extracting important molecules for energy, building and repair. Those that aren't utilized are stored as fat. We innately know which foods will serve us best at any given time and how to dine for optimum health. But we override our body's signals and often seek out "comfort" foods that have little nutritional value, but promise a break from boredom or stress. Consequently most people today really have no idea what constitutes a good diet and how to eat for optimum nutrition. Many people have allowed themselves to be controlled by food rather than controlling it. This lack of attention to innate wisdom about food flies in the face of eating patterns that have sustained humans for thousands of years. Choosing foods to maintain internal balance and adjust to climatic and seasonal changes has been practiced by all ancient cultures. The oldest healing systems in the world classified foods by color to emphasize their balancing effects and provide practical dietary guidelines. The Chinese Taoist tradition of nutrition is still useful today and provides a model for *7-Color Cuisine*.

The Tao of Nutrition

According to the 6,000-year-old Taoist tradition, the color of a particular food indicates its balancing and harmonizing effects. In the Taoist tradition, food keeps yin and yang energy in balance. Yin and yang have opposing effects, and having a balance between them is the way to achieve optimum health. Yin represents cooling and sedating effects while yang represents warming and energizing effects. Yin foods are purple, violet and blue in color and come primarily from plant sources. They have a soft quality and a cooling effect on the body. At the opposite end of the spectrum, yang foods are red and orange and have a quality of hardness and a warming effect on the body. Yellow and green foods are neutral in effect and balance the two extremes.

Tan foods, including whole grains, legumes, nuts, and seeds, are generally neutral in energy and help balance yin and yang. Tan foods are regarded even today as having stabilizing properties, and they have become the favorite target of food chemists who have processed and preserved all of the natural goodness out of these foods. Creamy white foods such as dairy products and oils are neutral in energy while fish, poultry, and meat tend to be warming, with red meat being highest in heat energy. In cold weather we add more of these high-protein foods to our meals. Although traditional practitioners didn't know about phytonutrients and zoonutrients, their dietary system provided the nutrients that heal the body and maintain homeostasis.

Eating predominately one color of food, especially the bland color of the typical Western diet, promotes imbalance within the body and, by extension, to the emotions and the mind. Happily, introducing a balance of colors as outlined in *7-Color Cuisine* will help offset the deleterious effects of a bland diet. If your diet is very bland, begin by adding some colors and new taste sensations each day as you take the first step to the full-spectrum eating of the 7-Color plan.

Using the Taoist understanding of food energy can help you select foods that are appropriate for the season, your mood, and your body's needs. For example, dark and cold winter months are more yin, and nature provides orange and red food in abundance during those times to counter yin extremes. Winter months also yield an abundance of garlic and cruciferous vegetables such as broccoli, cauliflower, and pungent mustard greens. These green foods promote circulation and reduce phlegm and congestion.

The Tao of nutrition reinforces the 7-Color wisdom of eating what's in season and choosing foods by color.

Enjoying the Taste of Food

Enjoying your meals takes time. No one savors his or her food on the run, so chew slowly and thoughtfully. Focus your attention on the textures and tastes of each bite. Notice when the individual flavors peak and when they blend with each other. Take note of the taste you're experiencing—salty, sour, sweet or pungent (like broccoli) that lingers the longest. Which one seems to titillate your taste buds? This can be a clue as to what's needed to balance your body, if you don't override the signals your body is sending. You may have to reeducate your taste buds if you've been eating primarily a bland diet. It doesn't take long, perhaps a week or two. And once you have awakened new taste sensations, bland food won't appeal to you any longer. You'll also find that food that's interesting to taste is more satisfying because it contains more nutrients.

Put your fork down frequently and just rest between bites. The first stage of digestion occurs in your mouth as salivary enzymes begin breaking down starches. Consequently chewing your food longer—especially food rich in carbohydrates—improves digestion. Someone once said you should "chew your food well, because your stomach doesn't have teeth." Although humorous, the statement bears truth. Anytime you improve your digestion and assimilation of nutrients, you're on the path to overcoming health challenges and promoting longevity and good health. Small meals count, too. Just remember that every time you put something into your mouth you're essentially enjoying a meal. Even snacks deserve your attention, so choose them carefully.

Mind, Body and the Metabolic Syndrome

In our rapid-paced society, mealtime is too often just a task to be checked off our daily to-do list. Breakfast is the most important meal of the day, yet many people don't eat breakfast. We're multitasking even before we head out the door to work, and we're lucky to cram something down as we watch the clock. Repeatedly grabbing something quick and eating under stress raises cortisol and insulin levels and alters glucose response. And that initiates a cascade of events that causes fat to be deposited in the abdomen. Physicians use the term "metabolic syndrome" to describe the process that often leads to chronic diseases such as diabetes and cardiovascular disease.

7-Color Cuisine makes allowance for weekday breakfasts with quick yet nutritious menus, reserving more elaborate meals for weekends. The combinations of foods you choose and the times you decide to eat your meals can be charted easily using the 7-Color plan.

Mindfulness: Improving the Assimilation of Nutrients

Cultivate an attitude of real appreciation for nature's bounty by absorbing the beauty of the food on your plate and reinforce an attitude of gratitude for the people involved in getting it in front of you. Be sure to compliment the cook and you'll be rewarded with more tasty meals. If you're the cook following the meal preparation guidelines in *7-Color Cuisine*, then your cooking efforts will have set the stage for obtaining optimum nutrition from the meal. Take a moment and admire your creation before picking up your fork. The awareness you cultivated while preparing the meal creates a deeper connection with your food.

Mindfulness and Intention

Without conscious intention we act from default programming, unaware of the digestive benefits of totally focusing on what we're eating. What are your intentions when you eat certain foods or certain meals? Is it to satisfy a craving for emotional comfort? Is it to provide a quick boost to your blood sugar? Or is it to nourish your body and spirit? Becoming clear about your intention before you eat will help you better obtain what you want from the food and is the first step toward weight management. "Getting it" that what you eat and how you prepare it does truly matter will erase the self-deception so common in our society that the next dietary regimen or pill will solve our weight concerns. Stating your intention before you eat even a single bite creates an inner calmness and connects you with the greater web of life.

Blessing Your Food and Companions

Connection is also an act of blessing your food, whether saying a prayer over your meal, holding your palms over the plate and sending energy to your food, or mentally sending thoughts of gratitude to the universe for providing emotional, mental, and physical nourishment. Your particular belief system is not the point. Awareness of what you're eating and where it came from is. Recent research points out that our thoughts affect digestion. Projecting blessings or thoughts of appreciation and gratitude onto your food is a simple but profound way to improve your health.

Raising the vibration of your food, in prayer or by another means, can help reduce the potentially harmful effects of eating less-than-healthy food or facing unavoidable circumstances, such as traveling or eating in unpleasant surroundings. Just learning to appreciate the colors of a well-balanced meal empowers you to lay the groundwork to improve your health. Taking time to appreciate each color of your meal enhances your enjoyment of each mouthful and the assimilation of each bite. And that translates into your absorption of more minerals, antioxidants, and vitamins to improve your immune system, repair damaged tissue, and replace old cells

Creating Ambience

Ambience refers to the atmosphere you create in which to enjoy your meals, with or without dining companions. Even if your dining companions are not as convivial as you might like, you can increase enjoyment of the meal by creating a spectacular environment. The beautiful meals you prepare using the 7-Color plan are designed to create excitement on your plate while you enhance the effect by choosing the location and setting a beautiful table. Doing so goes beyond lighting candles and playing soft music. Your idea of setting the scene for most relaxed and enjoyable eating could range from dining al fresco to a romantic dinner for two to a themed dinner party to breakfast in bed. What matters most is that you recognize how your surroundings affect food digestion and nutrient absorption.

To best savor your food you must sit comfortably in a setting that gives you quiet pleasure. Don't eat while standing and watching the clock. That's not eating; it's stuffing and usually means a mindless consumption of calories that does nothing for you nutritionally. Set the tone of your kitchen and dining area to eliminate rowdiness, distraction, or aggravation from family members when you eat. Turn off the disturbing news from the television, a common source of anger that can raise your blood pressure and stimulate the production of stress chemicals. The stress response shuts down the digestive process, as you read in the beginning of this book.

If you're dining alone, resist the temptation to accomplish something else at the same time. People who regularly dine alone tend to eat faster to get on to the next activity, or they read or watch television while they eat, forgetting about their meal as their interest is directed elsewhere. The best antidote for this habit is to fully execute all of the steps in *7-Color Cuisine*.

Finish your meals with a time of quiet reflection. Think what the word *savor* means to you and resist the urge to jump up from the table and move into another activity.

When to Quit Eating

Enjoying your food means eating until you feel satisfied rather than cleaning your plate. This is not an act of willpower, but an internal judgment from deep within your body. It's based on a variety of factors that come into play with your first mouthful of food. Weather, hormones, what and when you last ate, the amount of water in your body, the quantity and type of alcohol you've consumed, and the type of foods you're about to eat all have a big effect on how soon you'll feel satisfied from each meal.

Feeling satiated is not necessarily the same as feeling full. Satiety, also known as "intuitive eating," comes from the chorus your cells sing when receiving proper nourishment. Some food therapists even advise that you stop eating *before* you feel full and then wait a few minutes as your body begins processing the food you've already eaten. If you're listening for the satiety cue from your body, you won't overeat and you might just be surprised at how little it takes to reach satiety when you embrace the 7-Color Cuisine plan. Keep in mind that for most of us who live in this land of plenty there's always more food, if you really need it.

Intuitive Eating and Weight Management

Intuitive eating and setting the most appealing stage for eating are critical factors in effective weight management because they're not based on restrictive "can't" or "only" concepts common to dieting regimens. In June 2005 a research team at the University of California, Davis, reported that obese women were more successful in keeping weight off with a two-year healthy eating diet when they concentrated on learning intuitive eating instead of thinking how much weight they were losing. The women who ate the same, healthy diet but didn't practice intuitive eating lost weight the first year, but gained it all back in the second. You might find you're satisfied halfway through your meal without denying yourself any food from your plate. It's okay to push a half-full plate of food away. This one action improves your health and your waistline simultaneously. The concept of eating less, yet feeling more satisfied, is central to the 7-Color plan.

Nutritional science has also shown that digestive enzyme production is highest in people who stop eating when they feel less than full. The emotional state of satisfaction that accompanies satiety also relaxes the body and helps improve digestion. Once you've established the quantity of food that typically satiates, you can use portion control to measure the quantity of food you should consume at any one meal.

Portion Control

As children most of us heard the phrase, "your eyes must be bigger than your stomach," when we thought we could eat all the food we heaped on our plates Those of us who accepted the challenge and did eat it all were rewarded with serious indigestion for several hours after the meal. An individual's stomach should be the size of his or her fist, not the size of a dinner plate piled high with food. Eating to the point of satiety is the body's way of allowing room for digestive enzymes to circulate around what you've eaten, so use satiety as the measure of how nourishing your meal is and how much you've enjoyed it.

Using Condiments and Seasoning

Herbs and spices add interest to food and enhance the antioxidant effects of a meal. Most of the recipes in *7-Color Cuisine* use fresh herbs and powdered spices. Pepper is one spice you should routinely add to your food at the table. The phytonutrients in black pepper aid digestion and can be added to any dish or salad to enhance flavor. 7-Color recipes contain all of the salt you should consume in a day, so don't add salt at the table. And, unless the recipe calls for adding condiments or sauces, resist the temptation to slather your food with them. Let the full natural taste sensations of food delight your palate.

Beverage with Your Meal?

Drinking too much of anything with your meals, or before you sit down to a meal, dilutes digestive juices and hinders the digestive process. This is especially true of water, fruit juice, soda, beer, and cocktails. Except for small amounts of water and a little wine, liquids consumed before a meal just fill you up with liquid so that from your body's perspective, you're full before even before you start to eat. Water without ice, sipped during a meal, doesn't disrupt your digestion and, in some cases, may help make certain foods more palatable. The operative word here is *sipped*. Chugging water while you eat drowns your food, stops your digestion, and creates that bloated feeling.

There are many health benefits of enjoying wine with your meals, provided you have no specific health restrictions.

Dining Out

Enjoying your food when dining out involves choosing a restaurant that features fresh ingredients, preferably organic. To find a restaurant that features organic foods, go to Appendix D, the resource section of this book, for Web site addresses. To be certified as organic, a restaurant must offer only organic food, the premises must be maintained with organic cleaning products, and everything that comes into contact with food must be certified organic. The certification process is extremely time-consuming, because the USDA doesn't have clear guidelines on what constitutes certification for restaurants. Conscientious restaurateurs wind up having to help set standards. Restaurants that serve organic food but are not necessarily certified organic are becoming more widespread. However, in any restaurant you can't go wrong choosing those items that are freshest and in season. Once your meal arrives, evaluate the quality of ingredients on your plate. Decide what you want to eat at the table, what you might take home in a container, and what's best left behind. Practice the techniques you read about earlier in this chapter, taking special care to enjoy the new taste sensations offered by the chef. As in dining at home, be particularly aware of not overeating. Most restaurant food contains too much fat and too much sodium, but if you are careful about the amount you eat, you'll be okay.

Things to Avoid When Dining Out

A noisy hectic environment is not conducive to good digestion. Your attention is diverted from your meal by the distractions around you. If you want to eat at a popular "family style" restaurant, choose one that's relatively quiet.

Sports bars with televisions blaring are another example of a less-than-desirable environment. The fast-paced scenes, excessive volume, and negative subject matter of many television shows create a high-stress environment that can give you a serious case of indigestion. Airport cafes are springing up in response to lack of food service on many airlines. Some are located in relatively quiet food courts with comfortable seating or enclosed restaurants. They offer salads and fruit, a welcome change from airline meals. If you take food on the plane, try to create as much ambiance as you can and perhaps listen to music that you bring along or that's provided via airline headsets. Imagine that you are dining in first class on a transoceanic flight with all the amenities. That might be a stretch, but just give it a try!

Once you get the hang of the 7-Color Cuisine plan, all aspects of choosing and savoring food will become second nature to you. And please don't try to entertain your dining companions with your new awareness of how to enjoy food. Sharing a meal with someone is all about meeting a most basic human social need, and you don't want to disturb their dining experience (and their digestion) with a zealous or self-righteous attitude that begins with the "right" way to order from the menu. No one wants to eat with a fanatic, including me.

Dietary Supplements

As a nutritionist, I endorse the use of supplements in either of two ways: for health maintenance and to support the dietary plans in *7-Color Cuisine* as therapy to correct or prevent chronic conditions. A companion book, *7-Syndrome Healing*, rounds out a solid wellness program with dietary supplements for the mind and body.

Health Maintenance

We have reduced the amount of vitamins and minerals that we can get from our food due to depletion of nutrients in soil by recent agribusiness practices. Following the 7-Color system allows your body to obtain the nutrients you need mostly from the fresh food on your plate. The basic supplements described in Table 7-1 are meant for healthy adults and support the 7-Color plan. Please do not replace eating nutritious food by using supplements. Even the most balanced supplements miss hundreds of important phytonutrients and zoonutrients found only in food.

In addition, the 7-Color Cuisine plan includes whey protein powders (strawberry, vanilla, and chocolate) in many breakfast menus.

Organic raw food snack bars are also good supplement sources. They're usually made from berries; orange, yellow, and red tropical fruits; goji berries; green foods; and raw chocolate. They also include omega-3 bars.

Except for snack bars, always take supplements with a meal. The body is accustomed to processing hundreds of different nutrients in a meal, and the assimilation of vitamins and minerals will be enhanced.

TABLE 7-1 *Supplements by Color*

Color	Supplement Benefit	Supplement Examples
Red, orange, yellow	Fat-soluble antioxidant carotenoids, alpha and beta carotenes, lutein, and lycopene derived from broccoli, spinach, tomatoes, kale, cabbage, Brussels sprouts, asparagus, cauliflower, parsley, and carrots	Veggie Carotenoids, Caro-Plete
Purple	Water-soluble antioxidant polyphenols; anthocyanidin flavonoids, resveratrol from grape seed, grape skin, pomegranate, and green tea and enzogenol	Pomeratrol, Enzogenol, grape seed, grape-skin extracts, green tea extracts
Green	Supply multiple vitamins and minerals with green foods; spirulina, barley grass, chlorella, wheat grass with digestive enzymes to aid assimilation	Eco-Green Multiple, Alive Whole Food Energizer, Advanced Nutritional System
Tan	Vitamin E family of antioxidants stabilizes cells; supply vitamin E activity; alpha, beta, delta, and gamma tocopherols; and alpha, beta, delta, and gamma tocotrienols; octacosanol and phytosterols in the same ratios as naturally found in food	True E Complex from non-GMO soy, annatto, and virgin palm oils
White	Supply omega-3 and omega-6 fatty acids	Fish oil omega-3 capsules, liquid lemon omega-3 oil, and omega-3,6 organic snack bars

The 7-Color Companion Book

7-Color Cuisine contains all the dietary essentials for achieving optimum health. Its companion book, which has an emphasis on anti-aging, is *7-Syndrome Healing: Supplement Essentials for Mind and Body. 7-Syndrome* takes readers on an in-depth exploration that covers more than 130 of the most effective and beneficial dietary supplements, nutrients, herbs and other natural alternative remedies, all specifically tailored to address the following seven major wellness syndromes:

+ The Stress syndrome
+ The Metabolic syndrome
+ The Immune syndrome
+ The Cardiovascular syndrome
+ The Malabsorption syndrome
+ The Hormone syndrome
+ The Osteo syndrome

7-Syndrome Healing begins with a detailed discussion of the role of each vitamin and mineral needed to prevent deficiency symptoms. Optimum levels of these essential vitamins and minerals are given as the basis of a good supplement program. In discussing each of the syndromes, higher levels of a particular vitamin or mineral may be suggested, but always within the context of proper balance.

Additional nutrients are suggested for the various syndromes. Readers are treated with interesting historical facts, product overviews, supporting scientific evidence, potential drug interactions, natural companion supplements, helpful tips for taking each supplement, and much more.

Together, *7-Color Cuisine* and *7-Syndrome Healing* give you the perfect plan for living a healthy and vibrant life. And always remember to …

Take Pleasure in Life Today and Enjoy What You Eat!

Appendices

Identifying What You Need to Change

	Day 1	Day 2	Day 3	Day 4
Breakfast				
Snack				
Lunch				
Snack				
Dinner				
Snack				

For each day of the week, list what you ate, where you ate it (e.g., standing, at a table) and how you were feeling (e.g., sad, anxious). At the end of the week, circle the items you identify as unhealthy habits. They can be foods or the conditions under which you ordinarily eat.

Day 5	Day 6	Day 7

How to Read Nutrition Facts Panels

Macadamia Nut Oil

This is a nutrition facts panel from a bottle of macadamia nut oil.

Ingredients: Pure organic macadamia nut oil.

Minimize this kind of fat.

Trans fat is the worst kind of fat, must be listed in Nutrition Facts Panel by 2006.

Both poly- and monounsaturated fats are good forms of fat.

300 mg is the recommended daily value.

2400 mg is the recommended daily value.

Nutrition Facts

Serving Size: 1 Tbsp (15 ml)
Amount Per Container: 33

Amount Per Serving

Calories: 120   Calories from Fat: 120

% Daily Value*

Total Fat 14g	22%
Saturated Fat 2g	10%
Trans Fat 0g	
Polyunsaturated Fat 1g	
Monounsaturated Fat 11g	
Cholesterol 0mg	0%
Sodium 0mg	0%
Total Carbohydrates 0g	0%
Protein 0g	

Not a significant source of Dietary Fiber, Sugars, Vitamin A, Vitamin C, Calcium or Iron.

* Percent Daily Values are based on a 2,000 calorie diet.

Rolled Oats

This is a nutrition facts panel from a box of 5-Minute Rolled Oats. It is the gold standard for a breakfast cereal. Use this as a guide in comparing breakfast cereals. You will find that most have added sugar and salt, items you do not need.

Ingredient: whole grain oats.

Oatmeal is low in fat; most of the fat is unsaturated from the oat germ.

It contain no cholesterol or sodium, one of the reasons it is considered heart healthy.

Oatmeal is a rich source of fiber, both soluble and insoluble. It contains little sugar and none is added.

Although this is a carbohydrate-rich food, it also contains protein. Oatmeal's nutritional profile is typical of tan foods.

Oatmeal naturally contains iron. The product has not been fortified.

Nutrition Facts

Serving Size: ½ cup dry (40 grams)
Servings Per Container: 13

Amount Per Serving

Calories: 150   Calories from Fat: 25

% Daily Value*

Total Fat 3 g	13%
Saturated Fat 0.5 g	2%
Polyunsaturated Fat 1 g	
Monounsaturated Fat 1 g	
Cholesterol 0 mg	0%
Sodium 0 mg	0%
Total Carbohydrates 27 g	9%
Dietary Fiber 4 g	15 %
Soluble Fiber 2 g	
Insoluble Fiber 2 g	
Sugars 1 g	
Protein 5 g	

Vitamin A 0%	•	Vitamin C 0%
Calcium 0%	•	Iron 10%

* Percent Daily Values are based on a 2,000 calorie diet.

Organic Lentils

This is a nutrition facts panel from a can of organic black beluga lentils.

Ingredients: water, organic black beluga lentils, sea salt.

Legumes contain no fat or cholesterol.

This product is low in salt, even though some has been added.

Carbohydrates are lower in lentils than in whole grains such as oatmeal, yet they contain the same amount of fiber. They do not contain sugars.

Lentils and other legumes contain more protein than grains, making them an ideal source of this nutrient for vegetarians or for boosting protein intake.

Like grains, legumes are a rich source of iron.

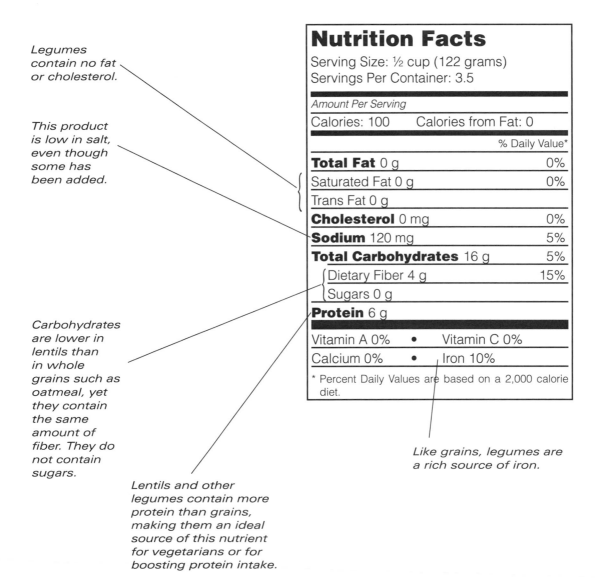

Nutrition Facts

Serving Size: ½ cup (122 grams)
Servings Per Container: 3.5

Amount Per Serving

Calories: 100   Calories from Fat: 0

% Daily Value*

Total Fat 0 g	0%
Saturated Fat 0 g	0%
Trans Fat 0 g	
Cholesterol 0 mg	0%
Sodium 120 mg	5%
Total Carbohydrates 16 g	5%
Dietary Fiber 4 g	15%
Sugars 0 g	
Protein 6 g	

Vitamin A 0%   •   Vitamin C 0%
Calcium 0%   •   Iron 10%

* Percent Daily Values are based on a 2,000 calorie diet.

Nonorganic Kidney Beans

This panel is from a can of nonorganic kidney beans and is used for comparison with the lentils.

Ingredients: prepared dark kidney beans, water, sugar, salt, calcium chloride, calcium disodium EDTA (to protect color)

Overall, the kidney beans have few calories and contain about the same amount of fat, protein. and carbohydrates as the lentils. However ...

... there is substantially more sodium in this product because of added salt,

... sugar has been added, and

... the calcium comes from preservatives.

Nutrition Facts

Serving Size: ½ cup (132 grams)
Servings Per Container: 2

Amount Per Serving

Calories: 100   Calories from Fat: 5

% Daily Value*

Total Fat 0.5 g	0%
Saturated Fat 0 g	0%
Trans Fat 0 g	
Cholesterol 0 mg	0%
Sodium 460 mg	19%
Total Carbohydrates 23 g	8%
Dietary Fiber 6 g	24%
Sugars 7 g	
Protein 7 g	

Vitamin A 0%	•	Vitamin C 0%
Calcium 8%	•	Iron 10%

* Percent Daily Values are based on a 2,000 calorie diet.

Shopping Lists

Cold Pantry

Dairy Products	Fish, Poultry, and Meat	Frozen Foods	Condiments and Dressings
• Low-fat milk • Soy milk, fortified (plain and flavored) • Yogurt, plain, low-fat • Kefir (low-fat liquid yogurt) • Cottage cheese, low-fat • Cream cheese, low-fat • Soft cheeses: ricotta, mozzarella, goat, jack, feta, bleu, low-fat soy • Hard cheeses for grating: Asiago, Parmesan, cheddar, Swiss • Sour cream, fat-free • Butter, salt-free • Margarine, soft, trans fat–free	• Salmon • Trout • White fish, turbot, scrod, cod, sole, calamari, grouper, etc. • Red snapper • Swordfish and tuna • Shellfish • Herring • Smoked salmon • Chicken • Turkey • Pork • Lunch meat, low-fat • Ham, fat-free • Sausage, low-fat • Beef, lean • Lamb, lean	• Unsalted organic petite green peas • Organic corn kernels • Blueberries • Strawberries • Blackberries • Cherries • Peaches • Select frozen entrées • Fruit juice–sweetened fruit bars • Fish, poultry, and meat kept on hand	• Balsamic vinaigrette • Raspberry vinaigrette • Red wine vinaigrette • Creamy ranch, low-fat • Bleu cheese, low-fat • Steak sauce, sugar-free • Salsa, fresh, sugar-free • Dijon mustard • Horseradish, freshly grated
TIPS: *Look for low-fat items and avoid synthetic dairy and cheese products. Buy organic milk products or those that do not come from hormone-treated cows.*	TIPS: *Check out the new choices of low-fat and reduced-salt meats. Buy wild Pacific salmon and trout whenever possible. Frozen fish can also be a good buy.*	TIPS: *Frozen fruit is generally picked and packaged at the height of the season. Look for and avoid products that contain added sugars. Look for low-salt frozen vegetables.*	TIPS: *Buy refrigerated or preservative-free dressings. Watch for added sugars and select those with the lowest salt content.*

Dry Pantry

Grains	Cereals	Flour Products	Nuts
• Amaranth • Barley • Brown rice: long-grain, short-grain, arborio, brown basmati, gourmet blends • Buckwheat groats (kasha) • Bulgur wheat • Couscous • Millet • Polenta (coarse cornmeal) • Quinoa • Wild rice or blends	• All bran • Corn flakes • Dry cereals, sugar-free • Granola, low-fat, no sugar • Kasha • Multigrain cereals • Old-fashioned oats • Smart Heart • Triticale flakes • Wheat flakes • Whole and cracked wheat	• Arrowroot • Buckwheat • Cornmeal • Flaxseed meal • Oat flour • Quinoa flour • Spelt flour • Teff flour • Wheat germ • Whole-wheat pastry flour • Whole-grain biscuit mix • Whole-grain pancake and waffle mix	• Almonds; whole, sliced • Brazil nuts • Cashews • Filberts • Macadamia nuts • Mixed nuts, unsalted • Pecans • Peanuts, unsalted • Pine nuts • Walnuts

Pasta	Crackers	Dry Beans	Seeds

• Angel hair
• Any whole-grain pasta, including:
  • buckwheat soba noodles
  • durum wheat semolina pastas
  • lasagna noodles
  • linguini; veggie, whole wheat
  • macaroni
  • orzo
  • penne ziti
  • rigatoni
  • smoked salmon farfalle
  • spaghetti
  • udon noodles; green tea, wheat
  • veggie pastas
	• Ak Mak
	• Flat bread
	• Kashi TLC
	• Lavash
	• Multigrain, no sugar
	• Rice thins
	• Sesame thins
	• Triscuits
		• Anasazi beans
		• Black turtle beans
		• Cranberry beans
		• Lentil and rice mix
		• Lentils: brown, pink
		• Mung beans
		• Split peas: green, yellow
			• Flax
			• Poppy
			• Sesame: black, white
			• Sunflower: raw, tamari

Dried Fruit, Unsulfured	Dried Vegetables	Chips	Breads
• Apples • Apricots • Cherries • Cranberries • Ginger, candied • Papaya • Peaches • Pears • Pineapple • Raisins • Trail mix: fruit and nuts only	• Bell peppers • Chili peppers • Mixed veggies, snacking • Tomatoes	• Blue corn chips, low-salt • Corn tortilla chips, low-salt • Wheat pita bread chips	• Naan, tandoori, wheat • Oatmeal • Tortillas: wheat, corn • Wheat pita • Whole multigrain • Whole wheat

Spices and Herbs

Spices and Herbs		Theme Combinations	
• Ajwain • Allspice • Anise seeds • Arrowroot • Basil • Bay leaves • Caraway seeds • Cardamom • Cayenne red pepper powder • Chili powder, medium hot • Chipotle peppers • Cinnamon sticks • Cinnamon, Vietnamese cassia • Cloves	• Coriander • Cumin, ground • Curry powder, hot • Dill weed • Epazote • Fennel • Ginger, crystallized • Ginger, powdered • Marjoram • Mignonette pepper • Mustard seed, yellow and black • Nutmeg • Oregano • Paprika, Hungarian half-sharp • Sage • Tarragon • Vanilla	• Barbecue seasoning • Bouquet garni • Cajun seasoning • Chesapeake Bay seasoning • Chili powder blends • Chinese five spice • Curry powder blends • Fines herbes	• Greek seasoning • Italian seasoning • Jerk seasoning • Mexican seasoning • Mulling spices • Poultry seasoning

Wet Pantry

Oils (Organic)	Vinegar (Organic)	Nut Butters (Organic)	Mustards and Pickles
• Almond • Canola • Extra virgin olive • Macadamia nut • Sesame, toasted • Walnut	• Balsamic, low acid • Raspberry • Red wine • Rice wine • White wine	• Almond • Cashew • Peanut • Sesame (tahini) • Sunflower seed	• Artichoke hearts • Capers • Dijon mustard • Flavored mustards, sugar-free • Fire-roasted green chilis • Olives, black and green • Pickles, dill, no sweeteners • Whole roasted sweet peppers

Canned Beans (Organic)	Canned Fish	Canned Vegetables	Fruit Juices
• Black turtle • Cannellini • Garbanzo • Kidney • Lentils • Refried, fat-free	• Clam juice (high in salt) • Clams, chopped, water-packed • Herring • Oysters • Sardines • Tuna, water-packed	• Artichoke hearts • Beets • Corn • Mushrooms • Pumpkin • String beans for salad	• Fresh fruit juices • Fresh protein smoothies • Unsweetened fruit juices

Jams and Sweeteners	Beverages	Aseptic Packs (Organic)	Specialty Items
• Fruit juice, sweetened • Fruit spreads • Honey • Maple syrup, pure • Molasses • Rice bran syrup	• Carrot juice • "Green" juices • Organic wines (optional) • Spritzers/club sodas • Teas: herbal, green, and black • Vegetable juices, low-salt • Water-processed decaf coffee	• Nut milk • Rice milk • Soups, organic • Soy milk	• Coconut milk, light • Sweetened condensed milk, low-fat

Resources

WEB ADDRESSES ARE given for the following companies so you can browse their products online. The products are available in natural foods stores and many supermarkets. Most offer products for online purchase, making it easy for you to obtain high-quality and organic products.

Barbara's Bakery
Petaluma, California
Organic breakfast cereals, cookies, crackers, and snacks
www.barbarasbakery.com

Bob's Red Mill Natural Foods, Inc.
Milwaukie, Oregon
Stone-ground natural, organic, and kosher whole-grain flours and mixes
www.bobsredmill.com

Eden Foods
Clinton, Michigan
Organic beans, pasta, condiments, soy milk, miso paste, sea vegetables, dried tomatoes, and nut butters
www.edenfoods.com

Hakubaku
Redondo Beach, California
Organic Japanese salt-free noodles
www.hakubaku.com

Horizon Organic and White Wave Organics
Boulder, Colorado
Certified organic dairy products, eggs, soy milk, soy products, juice, and Marie's Dips and Dressings
www.horizonorganic.com

Kashi Company
La Jolla, California
Cereals, bars, shakes, waffles, and crackers
www.kashi.com

R. W. Knudsen
Chico, California
Organic juices
www.knudsenjuices.com

Kozlowski Farms
Forestville, California
100% fruit spreads, syrups, marinades, fruit butters, salad dressings, and vinegars
www.kozlowskifarms.com

LocalHarvest (Organic Restaurants)
www.localharvest.org/restaurants/

Lodestar Farms
Oroville, California
Meyer lemon olive oil and California traditional late-harvest olive oil
www.lodestarfarms.com

Lundberg Family Farms
Richvale, California
Organic rice, rice cakes, pasta, and ready-to-cook side dishes
www.lundberg.com

MacNut Oil
Plano, Texas
*Unprocessed macadamia nut oil
from Australia*
www.macnutoil.com

Maranatha Nut Butters
Ashland, Oregon
Nut butters
www.nspiredfoods.com/ma-
ranatha.html

**Melissa's World Variety Pro-
duce**
Los Angeles, California
*Organic produce, herbs, and
specialty foods*
www.melissas.com

Nature's First Law
San Diego, California
Raw foods and raw chocolate
www.rawfood.com

NOW Foods, Inc.
Bloomingdale, Illinois
*Organic food products, snack
bars, whey protein powder,
dietary supplements, body care,
and essential oils and herbs*
www.nowfoods.com
www.now-2-u.com

Nutrition Express
Torrance, California
*Extensive line of supplements,
herbs, and body care products*
www.nutritionexpress.com

Odwalla
Half Moon Bay, California
Fresh juices and snack bars
www.odwalla.com

Organic Valley Family of Farms
La Farge, Wisconsin
*Certified organic butter, cheeses,
milk, meat, eggs, juice, soy, and
produce*
www.organicvalley.com

Organic Vintners
San Francisco, California
*Importer and distributor of
organic wines*
www.organicvintners.com

Organic Wine Company
San Francisco, California
*Importer and distributor of
organic wines*
www.ecowine.com

Penzey's Spices
Brookfield, Wisconsin
*Herbs and spices, 4/S salt, soup
bases, and theme seasonings*
www.penzeys.com

**Sierra Nevada Cheese
Company**
Organic Cheese Products
Willows, California
www.sierranevadacheese.com

Spectrum Organics
Petaluma, California
*Oils, dressings, and Spectrum
Essential Oils*
www.spectrumorganics.com

Stonyfield Farms
Londonderry, New Hamp-
shire
*Organic yogurt, smoothies,
cultured soy, ice cream, and
frozen yogurt*
www.stonyfield.com

Straus Family Creamery
Marshall, California
*Organic dairy products, cheese,
ice cream, and milk in glass
bottles*
www.strausmilk.com

Vital Choice Seafood
Bellingham, Washington
*Wild salmon (fresh, frozen, and
canned) and wild berries*
www.vitalchoice.com

Cooking Essentials

Stovetop, Grilling, and Steaming

- Stainless steel pots and pans with lids: 1-, 2-, 3-, and 5-quart
- Frying pans with lids: 8-inch and 10-inch
- Sauté pans: 8-inch and 10-inch
- Deep frying pan or wok: 12-inch
- Large roasting pan with rack
- Pressure cooker (e.g., Kuhn Rikon): 3½-quart for couples; 5-quart for families
- Indoor electric grill
- Electric griddle
- Electric steamer for vegetables and fish

Food Preparation Equipment

- Blender
- Food processor
- Electric mixer: stand or hand-held or both
- Salad greens spinner
- Mortar and pestle
- Chopping boards: 2 large and 2 small

Bowls

- Wooden salad bowl
- Small bowls, 4-ounce capacity: 6 to 8
- Small bowls, 6-ounce capacity: 4 to 6
- Large mixing bowls: one set

Knives

- Chef's knife: 7-inch
- Paring: two 3-inch (slim and thick blades)
- Utility: 5-inch medium and 4-inch small
- Carving: 8-inch
- Bread: 7-inch serrated
- Sharpening stone and steel for knives

Measuring Devices

- Glass measuring cups: 1-, 2-, and 4-cup sizes
- Nested, stainless measuring cups: ⅛-, ¼-, ⅓-, ½-, 1-, and 2-cup sizes (note: ⅛-cup size is a coffee measure)

- Stainless measuring spoons: ⅛, ¼, ½, ¾, 1 teaspoon, 1 tablespoon

Handy Gadgets

- Can opener
- Cheese grater
- Citrus zester
- Garlic press
- Ginger grater
- Hand citrus juicer
- Three-sided grater
- Vegetable peelers

- Spatulas, heatproof: 3 small, 3 medium, 2 large
- Spatulas, metal: 2 small, 1 medium, 1 large (some coated, as you prefer)
- Tongs, stainless: 2
- Soup and gravy ladles: small (½ cup), medium (1 cup), and large (1½ cups)

Miscellaneous

- Food storage containers of various sizes
- Kitchen towels and bar towels
- Pot holders and heat pads

Measurement Conversions

U.S. to Metric

Volume

- ¹/₅ teaspoon = 1 milliliter (ml)
- 1 teaspoon = 5 ml
- 1 tablespoon = 15 ml
- 1 fluid ounce (oz.) = 30 ml
- ¹/₅ cup = 50 ml
- 1 cup = 240 ml
- 2 cups (1 pint) = 470 ml
- 4 cups (1 quart) = 0.95 liter
- 4 quarts (1 gallon) = 3.8 liters

Weight

- 1 oz. = 28 grams
- 1 pound = 454 grams

Metric to U.S.

Volume

- 1 milliliter = ¹/₅ teaspoon
- 5 ml = 1 teaspoon
- 15 ml = 1 tablespoon
- 30 ml = 1 fluid oz.
- 100 ml = 3.4 fluid oz.
- 240 ml = 1 cup
- 1 liter = 34 fluid oz.
- 1 liter = 4.2 cups
- 1 liter = 2.1 pints
- 1 liter = 1.06 quarts
- 1 liter = 0.26 gallon

Weight

- 1 gram = 0.035 ounce
- 100 grams = 3.5 ounces
- 500 grams = 1.10 pounds
- 1 kilogram = 2.205 pounds
- 1 kilogram = 35 oz.

Cooking Measurement Equivalents

- 16 tablespoons = 1 cup
- 12 tablespoons = ¾ cup
- 10 tablespoons + 2 teaspoons = ⅔ cup
- 8 tablespoons = ½ cup
- 6 tablespoons = ⅜ cup
- 5 tablespoons + 1 teaspoon = ⅓ cup
- 4 tablespoons = ¼ cup
- 2 tablespoons = ⅛ cup
- 2 tablespoons + 2 teaspoons = $^{1}/_{6}$ cup
- 1 tablespoon = $^{1}/_{16}$ cup
- 2 cups = 1 pint
- 2 pints = 1 quart
- 4 quarts = 1 gallon
- 3 teaspoons = 1 tablespoon
- 48 teaspoons = 1 cup

Index

233

Brazilian Mocha Shake, 176, 188
Purple Passion Shake, 153, 159
Raspberry Parfait Shake, 175, 185
Strawberry Yogurt Breakfast Shake, 115, 121, 134, 155
Vanilla Peach Shake, 174, 181
Shell fish. See Fish
Shopping, 5–6
    for dairy products, 58
    for produce, 58–60, 78–79
    for sweeteners, 73
    trips per week, 56
    for whole grains, 61–62
Shopping lists, 5, 6, 56, 109, 220–223
    cold pantry, 220
    dry pantry, 221–222
    for salads, 85–88
    for spices and herbs, 222
    Week One, 118–120
    Week Two, 136–137
    Week Three, 156–158
    Week Four, 177–179
    wet pantry, 223
Shrimp with Sun-Dried Tomato Sauce, 173, 174, 180
Side dishes, 9, 52, 88. See also Rice
    Blanched Edamame with Slivered Almonds, 132, 135, 148
    Braised Winter Vegetables, 114, 117, 126
    Butternut Squash and Kale Sauté, 173, 176, 190
    Fruit Cup with Yogurt, 129, 173, 175
    Garlic Mashed Potatoes, 132, 134, 144
    Golden Couscous with Parsley and Green Peas, 132, 133, 139
    Green Beans with Almonds and Roasted Red Bell Peppers, 153, 155, 166
    Orange-Glazed Carrots and Parsnips, 153, 156, 170
    Spring Asparagus and Fennel Sauté, 153, 154, 162
    Steamed Asparagus with Tarragon and Lemon, 173, 177, 196
    Stir Fry Vegetable Medley, 23, 28
    Stir-Fried Vegetables with Toasted Cashews, 173, 176, 187
    Summer Vegetable Grill, 132, 135, 151
Slow food movement, 11–12
Smokers, benefits of plan for, 50–51

Snacks, 22, 29–30, 52–55, 200
    cheeses, 58
    in daily menu plans, 77, 109
    dried vegetables and fruit, 29–30, 70
    green vegetables, 35
    miso soup, 63
    organic raw food snack bars, 210
    tan foods, 38
Sodium, 13, 29, 92–93. See also Salt
Soft drinks, 13, 64
Sole with Avocado Lime Cream, Tequila, 132, 133, 138–139
Sorbitol, 65, 66
Sorrel Sauce, Scallops with French, 153, 154, 160–161
Soups, 16, 41
    beans in, 73
    Ginger Orange Soup, 96, 97, 153, 154, 163
    Golden Chicken Soup, 114, 116, 122
    Leek and Potato Soup, 23, 24
    for main course, 88, 96
    miso, 63
    modules, 97
    Purple Borscht Soup with Beef, 96, 97, 173, 174, 182
    Red Hungarian Soup, 97, 98–99
    7-Color Minestrone, 97, 104–105
    Split-Pea Soup with Ham, 132, 133, 141
    Yellow Curry Soup, 97, 101
    Zesty Green Soup, 97, 102
Soy milk, 58, 71, 106–107, 223
Soy nuts, 81, 83, 86
Soy products, 22, 40, 85, 210. See also Miso
Soy sauce, 41, 71
Soybeans, 62, 63
    Blanched Edamame with Slivered Almonds, 132, 135, 148
Specialty items, 223
Spices. See Herbs and spices
Spinach, 59, 79, 80, 82, 85
    organic, 18
    steaming, 15
    Wilted Spinach and Orange Salad, 132, 133, 140
Squash, 59
    Butternut Squash and Kale Sauté, 173, 176, 190
Starches, 22, 32–33

Steamed food
    green vegetables, 15, 35
    Steamed Asparagus with Tarragon and Lemon, 173, 177, 196
    Steamed Brown Rice, 95, 114, 118, 120
    Steamed Salmon with Tarragon and Lemon, 23, 26
    steamer, use of, 30, 226
    whole grains, 61
Stevia, 66
Stew, 88
    Savory Beef Stew, 132, 134, 145
Stir fry
    macadamia nut oil used for, 90
    for main course, 88
    Stir Fry Vegetable Medley, 23, 28
    Stir-Fried Vegetables with Toasted Cashews, 173, 176, 187
Stovetop cooking, 226
Strawberries, 59, 82, 86
    Strawberry Yogurt Breakfast Shake, 115, 121, 134, 155
Stress, lowering, 5, 13, 16, 33, 201, 203–204
Sugar, 20, 38, 39, 55, 64–66
    in canned foods, 72
    in condiments and sauces, 71
    in dried fruits, 71
    forms of sugar in foods, 41
    natural, 65–66
    in salad dressings, 41
Sulfites, 75, 76
Sulfur, 34–35
Summer foods
    salads, 80, 108
    Summer Vegetable Grill, 132, 135, 151
Sunflower seeds, 81, 83, 86, 109
Super Salad. See Salads
Sweeteners
    natural, 65–66
    shopping for, 73, 223
    synthetic, 55, 64–65, 72
Swordfish with Chipotle Salsa, Grilled, 173, 177, 193–194
Tan dietary supplements, 211
Tan foods, 29, 36–39, 199
    for breakfast, 106
    shopping list, 119, 136, 156, 177
Tangerines, 80, 82, 86
Tao of nutrition, 21–22, 198–200
Tarragon, 88

Pan-Seared Wild Pacific Salmon
with Tarragon Aioli, 114, 118, 127–128
Steamed Asparagus with
Tarragon and Lemon, 173, 177, 196
Tea, 34, 74–75
Tomatillos, 80
Tomato juice, 23
Tomatoes, 31, 59
canned, 72
Chicken-and-Turkey Sausage with
Sun-Dried Tomatoes, Purple
Cabbage, and Red Apples, 114,
118, 130
marinated, dried, 70
in salads, 80, 82, 86
in season vs. out-of-season, 17
Shrimp with Sun-Dried Tomato
Sauce, 173, 174, 180
storage of, 60
Traveling, eating when, 8, 209. See
also Restaurant meals
Tuna, 72, 223
Country Tuna Pie, 153, 155, 167–168
Lime-and-Ginger-Seared Ahi Tuna,
114, 115, 121
Turkey, 40, 220
Mediterranean Meat Loaf,
132, 134, 143
U.S. Department of Agriculture
(USDA), 16–17, 66
Food Guide Pyramid, 20
organic restaurants, certification
process for, 207
organic wines, labeling of, 76
U.S.-metric conversions, 228
Vegetable juices, 73, 106–107, 223
Vegetable pasta. See Pasta, whole
grain or vegetable
Vegetables, xviii, 20
alkaline-buffering minerals in, 12
for breakfast, 106–107
canned, 72–73, 223
Chicken Basmati Rice with Garden
Vegetables and Herbs, 173, 175,
183–184
Creamy Risotto with Vegetables,

114, 117, 125
dried vegetables, 70–71, 222
freezer storage of, 60
green, 32, 36, 37
Linguini with Vegetable Sauté, 68–69
for lunch, 77, 107–108
orange, 32
pasta, served with, 67–69
purple, blue, and black, 34, 35
Rainbow Chicken Salad, 153, 156, 171
red, 31
in salads, 79–81, 82
sea vegetables, 41–42
shopping for, 58–59, 85–86, 222, 223
side dishes (See Side dishes; Soups;
specific vegetables)
snacks, 30, 35, 77, 109
in soups, 96
Spring Halibut Sauté with
Vegetables and Linguine, 173,
176, 189
storage of, 57–60
Vegetable Omelet, 176, 191
yellow, 33
Vegetarian diet, 61, 67
Vinegar, 74, 223
in salad dressings, 83, 84, 87
storage of, 88
Vitamin A, 32, 58, 73
Vitamin C, 17, 35, 73
Vitamin E, 36, 88, 211
Vitamins
in green foods, 34, 35, 36
in raw foods, 15
supplements, 210–212
in tan foods, 36
Walnut oil, 83, 84, 87
Walnuts, 69, 81, 83, 86
Water, 14, 54, 206–207
Watermelon, 31
Web addresses, food resources, 224–225
Weekends, menu plans for, 109–110
Weekly plans. See Menu plans
Weight, xvii, 29
breakfast and, 106
fad diets, use of, 50

mindfulness, effect of, 202
motivation for plan use, 48
pasta and, 67
tan food and, 39
when to quit eating (satiety), 204–206
Wet pantry, 56, 71–76, 118
Whey protein powder, 106–107, 210.
See also Shakes, breakfast
White dietary supplements, 211
White foods. See Creamy white foods
Whole grains, xviii, 20, 38, 77, 199. See
also Breads
breakfast foods, 106–107
cooking, 61–62
flours, 60, 64, 221
fresh vs. rancid, 62, 64
pasta (See Pasta, whole grain
or vegetable)
shopping for, 61–62, 221
side dishes, 88
storage of, 60, 61, 62, 64
Wine, 75–76, 206–207
Winter foods, 199
Braised Winter Vegetables, 114,
117, 126
salads, 80–81
vegetables, 32, 59, 199
Wolfe, David, 14
Xylitol, 65, 66
Yams, 59, 73
Yellow dietary supplements, 211
Yellow foods, 22, 29, 33–34, 199
Yellow Curry Soup, 97, 101
Yin and yang of foods, 21–22, 198–200
Yogurt
for breakfast, 23, 106–107
Fruit Cup with Yogurt, 118, 129,
156, 173, 175
in salad dressings, 84
shopping for, 58
as snack, 109
as soup topping, 96
Strawberry Yogurt Breakfast Shake,
115, 121, 134, 155
Zeaxanthin, 34
Zoonutrients, xvi, 4, 21